GHOST BROTHER ANGEL

GRANT SCHNARR

GHOST BROTHER ANGEL

Swedenborg Foundation Press

West Chester, Pennsylvania

Library of Congress Cataloging-in-Publication Data
Schnarr, Grant R.
Ghost brother angel / Grant Schnarr.
p. cm.
ISBN 978-0-87785-346-6 (alk. paper)
1. Schnarr, Grant R.   2. Swedenborgians—
Biography.   I. Title.
BX8749.S36A3 2012
289'.4092—dc23
[B]
2012011881

Edited by Morgan Beard
Text design and typesetting by Kachergis Design

Printed in the United States of America

Swedenborg Foundation Press
320 North Church Street
West Chester, PA 19380
www.swedenborg.com

In memory of Jason—

a steadfast spiritual

warrior

CONTENTS

Preface   ix

PART 1. HAUNTED

1. The Ghost in the New Room   3

2. Caution!   11

3. Is This the End?   20

4. Aftershock   28

PART 2. AFRICAN AWAKENINGS

5. Survivors   37

6. Trauma   48

7. Hoka Hey!   58

8. Run into the Roar   70

9. I Can't Believe This Is Happening!   79

PART 3. LACHY BROWN

10. Home? 91

11. Laurel Camp 98

12. A Push from Beyond 107

13. Silver Star 114

14. A Circle of Brothers 130

PART 4. ENCHANTED FOREST

15. The Northwoods 145

16. Love and Fear 155

17. Afraid of the Deep 167

18. Guideposts and Guardians 177

19. My Big Brother! 186

20. Signs 195

PART 5. HOME!

21. Still Reaching 205

22. Connecting the Pieces 214

23. Reunited 225

Addendum 239

PREFACE

Were you afraid of the dark as a child? Who hasn't experienced that slight chill down the spine when the lights go off? When I was little, it wasn't just the dark I was afraid of—it was what the dark represented. It was something deeper and more terrifying. It was the void, the empty spaces in my life. Years later, I realized that those fears weren't just random. I was being haunted.

I wrote this story down right after it happened in 1996. I had to. The events that took place, the series of "coincidences" that happened so rapidly and with such spiritual purpose and consequence were beyond even what many call "serendipity." I found my situation and experiences during this time to be nothing short of astonishing.

This is a true story, and true stories are not fairy tales taking the reader down a single path to resolution. True stories unfold as they will. Though I changed some names and adapted a number of incidental details to preserve the integrity of the storyline, I want to take you through the journey exactly as it happened to me, through a string of seemingly unrelated events: a terrifying airplane flight, a trip through some dark parts of South Africa, a meeting in a church camp in western Pennsylvania, revelations in the solitude of the Northwoods of Wisconsin, and finally coming home, truly coming home. At the time I did not recognize an undeviating thread of purpose and resolution in these events, but now that I look back, more than fifteen years later, I see that everything happened with a single and momentous purpose, one that led to a realization of the power of spirit, and humanity, and love, both as we experience it in this world and, yes, in the unseen world to come.

The story truly began when I was a child, with that fear of the dark, of the empty spaces, from the space under my bed to the closets in my room. Some part of me felt that there was something in that void, anonymous, chilling, wanting to reach me. There were two closets in my room that faced each other, and I was sure there was something very frightening in them, some kind of monster that could come barreling out at night, or maybe even in the day. I'd take my wooden toy blocks and arrange them in such a way that I created a wedge to block both doors from opening. Now that I think of it, I was terrified of every closet, of what might have been hiding behind the clothes hanging there. I was afraid of the basement, the attic—anywhere there were dark places and empty spaces.

Though I grew up with four sisters—Beth Ann, Sue, and Linda were older than me and Melanie was two years younger—I spent most of my childhood alone. Melanie and I would occasionally play with building blocks together, or I would enlist her to make an opposing army out of those three-inch plastic solders every boy had in the sixties, and we would roll golf balls across the carpeted floor in my bedroom to see who could win by knocking down the other's forces first. We'd talk sometimes, but in childhood she always seemed to be frail and emotionally fragile. I couldn't put a name to my impressions as a child, but I knew that playing together often raised a certain level of anxiety within me. I couldn't have told you why or what that anxiety was. I just knew that as we played—and in my memory it was always in a dark room or on a gloomy, rainy day—I felt more alone inside. I sensed her loneliness and sense of vulnerability, and it only increased my own. It seemed like the empty void was always just around the corner. It would often descend and envelop us as we tried to lose ourselves, or at least our feelings, in childhood play.

We truly did spend our early childhood alone. When we were toddlers my oldest sister, Beth Ann, cared for us, singing us bedtime songs and waiting till we were asleep before turning off the bedroom lights and leaving us. As we got older, she moved on to college. Our other two sisters spent their high school days, as is completely understandable, off hunting boyfriends and being quite successful at it. They were preoccupied with their own lives. Dad worked till six every day, and he was also very often away for days on end on business trips, which most of the time left us alone with our mother.

I can't say that my mother wasn't always with us. She stayed home practically all the time. She kept herself busy in the house cleaning, folding wash, or working hard at doing some chore to keep the house neat and tidy. We didn't really see much of her. It's not that she wasn't there, but looking back now I realize she really *wasn't there* emotionally. I can say for myself that I always felt that she loved me, but her love was shrouded in a type of sadness. The only time that love seemed to break free and reach out to me was when my asthma would flare up full force, or when I was sick with a bad flu. She stopped everything to care for me with a fierce determination, as if she were obsessed with doing anything and everything possible to get me better. Back then I saw it as love, and I still believe it truly was, but at the core of that love sat a silent, volcanic fear, and it drove her in times like these. Her fear seemed natural to me. I was a sickly child, and I spent a handful of lengthy stays in the hospital with pneumonia, or croup, or a bad case of asthma. She would take me to the doctor practically once a week for a shot of antibiotics. I slept with a vaporizer by my bed. The noise of that vaporizer humming along every night gave me such comfort; even to this day I still use a fan or one of those noise machines to help me sleep. I suppose the noise of the vaporizer sang to me that I was indeed loved, safe, and secure. Mom showed her true self most, and seemed to love me most, when I was sick.

In my mind's eye I can go back to those times in an instant. I felt a tangible fear of the darkness and void most strongly when I was ill and apparently at death's door. There was one particular Christmas night when I was in our family room bouncing around on my new child-sized trampoline. As I stepped off the trampoline I distinctly remember a sense of doom rising up within me as the room grew dark and my chest grew tighter and tighter. A combination of croup and asthma had gripped my lungs. My parents called our family doctor (they used to make house calls back then), and I was scooped up, covered in a wool blanket, and rushed to the hospital. At the hospital they discovered I had a bad case of pneumonia. I remember wondering to myself whether this was the night I would disappear into that deathly void, never to return.

I often had that sense of doom in the family room, which our family called the New Room. It never seemed to leave. I didn't understand it as a child, but it became clear to me as I grew into adolescence. The room was haunted.

PART 1

HAUNTED

1

THE GHOST IN THE
NEW ROOM

Yes, I was afraid of the darkness, ghosts, and the void in childhood. But that didn't mean some of those ghosts weren't real. Let me start from the beginning.

In 1963, my parents, Ronnie and Bette Schnarr, with four daughters and one son (me) between the ages of one and fifteen, decided to expand our house. They built a new garage and turned the old one into a recreational room. It was very modern by the standards of the time, with wood paneling and a drop ceiling, bay window, fireplace, wet bar, stereo, piano, two large sofas, end tables, chairs, and so on. Since it was the newest room in the house, our family called it the New Room.

The New Room was large, and because of this we would celebrate Christmas there, decorating the room and setting up the tree; on Christmas morning we would find our filled stockings hanging from the beautiful stone fireplace when we came to open our gifts. It was also used for entertainment, and the children would hang out there with their friends. It was separated from the rest of the house by a long hallway with doors on either end, so it was very private.

The room didn't look haunted. Nothing about it appeared in the remotest sense scary, except perhaps for the old deer head mounted on the wall next to the fireplace, staring down on those who entered. Dad had bagged that deer years earlier and was very proud of his trophy. The really unnerving part about the room was what would happen there.

I grew up knowing that there was something different about that room. There always seemed to be some sort of presence there. The presence would sometimes be very strong, as if something was going to appear to one of us if we stayed too long. I always had a sense that it was sad and gloomy, especially on Christmas night after the presents had been opened, dinner had been served, and the darkness of winter set in. It sounds trite, but the presence was so thick that you could cut it with a knife. One Christmas, my sister Sue, who was around twelve at the time, went to play in the room while all were busy elsewhere in the house. She heard a peculiar noise, as if someone were either laughing or crying, and it seemed to be getting louder. She thought it must be coming from the house next door, so she went to the window and opened it. At that point she realized that the sound, which was growing louder, was coming from the room itself. She ran in fear.

My sisters regularly complained that they felt like they were being watched by someone when they sat in that room with their boyfriends. Perhaps my father was checking up on them through some shifty, covert means, but I don't think so. They swore that there was a presence in the room with them, and it would become so powerful and unnerving that they and their boyfriends would be forced to leave. It became too frightening to stay. Growing up, I had this same experience when I used to practice the trumpet in that room by myself. The presence would become so strong, looming right behind me, that I finally had to put the trumpet down and run out, not looking back.

In my teenage years, my friends and I began to toy with the paranormal and actually tried to make friends with the "ghost." We held a séance, and nothing happened at that time, but soon afterward we felt we had made contact through a very peculiar means. My parents had bought an old RCA record player, which was mounted on the wall in one corner of the room. When we played records in that room, we noticed that the ghost liked certain songs and didn't like others. With some songs, the presence would become very strong, almost to the point of appearing. On the other hand, when we played songs the ghost didn't like, the room filled with agitation. For instance, the ghost liked "Tuesday Afternoon" by the Moody Blues. It hated "Wild Thing" by The Troggs. There was an electrical short in the record player, so occasionally it would give out a loud, screeching noise through the speakers. It seemed to happen randomly, but then we realized, in our innocent—or should I say ignorant and childlike—way, that the screeching wasn't always random. Sometimes it was, but sometimes it was purposeful and creepy. If the ghost didn't like a song, it would make the record player screech. When it screeched, we'd yell, "Shut up!" It would stop right on cue. This happened time and again. It was sort of a game. The ghost seemed to play with us, and we played with it, through the stereo.

This came to a head one day when my friend Mark and I were sitting next to the stereo listening to "Wild Thing." The 45 rpm record of "Tuesday Afternoon" sat right above it on the disc, ready to come down and play next. To our amazement, the room suddenly filled with agitation. Something moved in the direction of the record player. Both of us watched from less than two feet away as the arm of the record player rose. "Tuesday Afternoon" was lifted up in the air and the needle raced and scratched across "Wild Thing." Then the "Wild Thing" record lifted off the player, flew across the room, hit the fireplace, and broke into pieces. "Tuesday Afternoon" gently came back down onto the record player, the needle set onto the record, and the song began to play. We screamed. We ran. We cried in terror as we told my parents. But, like many ghost stories, there wasn't much we could do about it. We weren't hurt, so we sort of forgave the ghost and let it go. We stayed away from the room for a few weeks, but eventually wandered back in. I remember saying to myself a hundred times, maybe even a thousand times, that this couldn't have happened! But it did. It defied all the laws I had been taught, but it happened, and all I could do is accept that some weird things happen. We just had to live with it.

Living with it became fairly easy. In fact, my best friend and I spent so much time in that room, doing homework, listening to records, watching television, or talking, that we both became skilled at knowing exactly what part of the room the presence was occupying at the time. In our college years, a student who was doing a thesis on the paranormal came in to do some research on this phenomenon of the New Room. In a controlled experiment, my friend and I were able to independently pick out where the ghost was in the room nine out of ten tries.

The presence wasn't all bad, either. My youngest sister and I both agreed that when we were sad about something as teenagers—perhaps over a lost love, or some conflict with a friend—and we'd go into that room to listen to music and lament, the ghost would come and try to comfort us. It seemed as if sadness was its specialty, and if we were sad, it was there to empathize and even to console.

Whatever the ghost was, whatever it wanted, the scariest thing about it was that we felt it was always just on the verge of appearing. It would often concentrate its activity near the doorway. Twice in my later teen years I saw it open a door. Once I informed my mother I was going into the New Room to play the guitar. She told me not to play too loudly because the neighbors had complained. I smiled, pulled the hall door shut behind me, walked down the hall, pulled the second door shut behind me as I entered the New Room, turned on the amp full blast, and began to play. I stood in front of the door with a big smile on my face, knowing my mother would soon enter to tell me to turn it down. I watched as the doorknob turned, and I watched with a smile as it swung open. But my smile slowly faded into puzzlement and concern. No one was there. The door had opened itself—or something other than a living human being opened it.

A few years later, the same thing happened in a different circumstance. I was expecting a friend to come through the door, and I watched the door open, but there was no one there—at least, no one living.

At one time I actually thought that maybe I was causing the paranormal phenomena. In the two cases I just described I was expecting the door to open. I had heard somewhere that usually when there is a poltergeist in the house, you will find a disturbed adolescent living there, and that there is some sort of energy given off by this adolescent. Since I was getting in trouble with the law at that time—breaking into houses, drinking, smoking, that sort of thing—perhaps I was unconsciously moving objects with some sort of psychic power stemming from my repressed anger. I was definitely running from something at the time. Alcoholism in the family? Parental discord? The loneliness of that house? Maybe I was the one disturbing this home.

I don't want to make it sound as if everything was bad with our family. We had plenty of good times, and I had friends over constantly. A couple of my friends still think of my mother and father as surrogate parents. The Schnarr house was a friendly, busy place. However, it is also true that something deeply troubling was under the surface, trying to get out. To all outward appearances things were fine, but perhaps all those unsettling impulses that had been pushed beneath the surface and compartmentalized were now locked into a certain room in the house—the New Room. I was intrigued with the idea. I later discarded this theory when I actually saw someone in the room.

One night I was "watching television" alone in the New Room with my girlfriend, Alice. We were both juniors in high school at the time. My parents had told me to leave the door open, so I had it ajar about an inch, and I kept my eye on it as we sat on the couch. At one point I looked over at the door and saw a man standing there. He appeared to be in his twenties, wearing dark blue pants and a red shirt. The scary thing was that he had no face. Above his shoulders was simply a silhouette of a head, and a faint blurry glow replaced any facial features. As soon as I saw him, he slipped away through the one-inch crack in the door.

I jumped up and yelled as every hair on my body stood on end. I grabbed Alice by the arm and we both ran out the very doorway where I had seen the apparition not moments earlier. Again I went to my parents, frightened and excited, and told them what I had seen. They just seemed perplexed and bewildered. They didn't believe in ghosts. Even when strange things happened to them in the New Room, they simply made up some explanation, not wanting to admit the possibility of something from another world. I wanted to find an explanation, too, but there simply wasn't one that fit the laws of nature. You could argue that it was my imagination, but at the time I wasn't thinking about seeing a man in his twenties, or about the ghost. I was busy doing other things!

What makes this story even more intriguing is what happened the next morning. Alice came over early and we decided to go back into the New Room, to reclaim it for ourselves. As we entered the room we both saw that the deer head up on the wall had fallen to the middle of the floor. Alice fell to her knees and shrieked, "Oh no! Oh no! I can't believe it!" She was shaking.

"Last night," she went on to explain, "when you continued to talk to your mother about the ghost, I came back in here to get my shoes. I sat down on the couch and looked at the deer head on the wall, and I challenged the ghost. I said, 'If there is a ghost in here, let this deer head fall. If there is a ghost in here, let this deer head fall!'" We both looked at each other in dazed disbelief as the deer head lay on the ground before us. We left the room once more. How could this be? What was this about? We didn't know.

As I grew older, I did some research to see if the room had been built over a graveyard, or perhaps an Indian burial site. Nothing turned up. Another friend, Jim Turner (one of the many believers who had experiences with the ghost himself), and I cut a hole into the crawl space above the New Room and explored the entire area to see if maybe my dad or perhaps the builder had hidden a body up there. We didn't think so, but it was worth a look. It turned out that the only thing hidden up there were some beer cans from the builders. Why this room seemed to be haunted remained a mystery to all of us children as we grew up and one by one left the house.

Later on my parents converted the New Room into an apartment. They added two rooms at the back and divided the New Room into a living room and kitchen. The woman who lived there for several years is the mother of a famous director and grandmother to two successful movie actors. She never heard or felt anything strange in the apartment. Years later, as fate would have it—and who says God doesn't have a sense of humor?—we now own the house, and my mother-in-law lives in the apartment.

The ghost in the New Room was a reality in my childhood and teen years. It was one of those things in life that never made sense—sort of a question mark and a shrug of the shoulders about my early years. As I grew to adulthood and became a husband and a father myself, I forgot about it. Then something happened to bring the memory back, and that memory would prove vital to solving one of the biggest puzzles of my life.

2

CAUTION!

My wife, Cathy, and I sat in a crowded terminal at John F. Kennedy airport in New York on a hot afternoon in May 1996, waiting to board South African Airways Flight 102 to Johannesburg, South Africa. It was our first trip overseas together. We would be away from our four children—Ronnie (15), Jason (13), Owen (11), and Steven (9)—for more than two weeks.

Cathy is an extremely attractive woman, if I do say so myself, with medium-length brown hair, blue eyes, and a killer smile. She was excited about the trip and also apprehensive about being away from the kids, as any mother would be. She had placed each of our children with families near our home in Bryn Athyn, Pennsylvania, just outside of Philadelphia. She had given each a care package of goodies and about four pages of instructions for the parents who would be caring for them. She shed a lot of tears when she left the children.

"Do you think they'll be OK?" she asked as she

checked her bag one more time to ensure she had their telephone numbers in case of emergency.

"I think they'll be fine. I'm worried about us," I replied with a half smile.

"Don't take me there, Grant. I'm not going if you start filling me with worries again."

"OK. I'll stop. I think everything will be fine."

I wasn't really lying, but I had a good deal of anxiety about this trip. It was supposed to be fun and exotic—a once-in-a-lifetime business trip to Africa where my wife could come along on the church's expense account. I was a minister and the director of evangelism for the worldwide New Church. The New Church, often called "Swedenborgian," is a Christian church based on the teachings of the eighteenth-century scientist and theologian Emanuel Swedenborg. His teachings are a very commonsense approach to life, emphasizing a loving God and living a useful life. He also offers one of the most extensive descriptions of heaven and hell—something that attracted and influenced a lot of artists, authors, philosophers, and religious leaders throughout history. In fact, Raymond Moody, in his breakthrough book about near-death experiences, *Life after Life,* refers to the "astounding" similarities between Swedenborg's descriptions of the afterlife and the accounts of those who have had a near-death experience. I find that Swedenborg's vivid descriptions of the afterlife and his positive view of life in general excite the imagination and spur creativity.

Because of Swedenborg's strong teachings about the reality of a "spiritual world" and his background in Christianity, his teachings are quite popular in Africa, where one often finds a combination of Christian thought as well as a strong belief that we are connected to the world of spirit and the afterlife. On this particular trip, I was embarking on an ambassador-type visit to meet a variety of our church congregations in both the white and black districts of South Africa. I had heard the country was incredibly beautiful, and the people from South Africa I had met over the years were certainly special—robust and delightfully cheerful. They looked forward to welcoming us, and we would be treated like royalty everywhere we went. They even planned a safari for us at the end of our business.

Part of my worry was the worsening political situation in South Africa. Apartheid had ended, which was wonderful for all, but the expectations of the people were extremely high. Unrest was growing, and with it, incredibly vicious crime. We would not only be staying in heavily fortified homes in the white districts, where crime had risen—Johannesburg, for example, had one of the highest murder rates in the world—but we would also be visiting the townships and staying in Soweto, deep in the heart of the trouble. It was an area where most white men don't get to go, and many choose not to go because of the racial hatred and unrest. The vast majority of the South African people were law-abiding, good-natured citizens, but there were also thugs and killers.

Hearing about the growing trouble, I had placed a long-distance call to one of the pastors in Durban, South Africa. I had heard that violence against women was rising, and wanted to quell my fears about bringing Cathy along. I asked the pastor, "They're into carjacking now, I hear. So, all Cathy and I have to do is keep a hand on the door handle, and when they come to steal the car, we just get out and let them take it, right?"

"It's not that easy, Grant. They'll let you out, but they won't let her out. In fact, they'll drive off and do terrible things to her before they kill her." By the tone of his voice, I knew he was completely serious.

My heart in my throat, I responded, "Should I bring her, then?"

"Oh, sure. The chances of that happening are slim. Anyway, it would be a comfort to the ministers' wives over here to see her brave the trip. Really, it should be OK. You just have to have a plan in case there is trouble. Really, she must come. I'm just giving you the worst of it. She'll be fine. Everyone's excited she's coming!"

I told Cathy about the conversation, having pretty well made up my mind that I did not want her to go. But she insisted, pointing out that a lot of church members lived there and many had never had anything violent happen to them. The pastors' wives were looking forward to her visit, and what would they think if she didn't come? She assumed the pastor I'd spoken to was exaggerating, and knew for certain that I was. We agreed that she would go, but we did have a plan. If carjacked, I divert, she runs, and then I run. Our motto to live by while we were over there was "Better to be shot than to be taken." That resolved the dilemma, though I must confess that this little motto didn't bring much comfort.

But the other problem I had with this trip was that I didn't like to fly. My job required me to fly fairly often to various congregations around North America, but I didn't like it. And at that time this particular direct flight to South Africa was the longest flight in commercial aviation history, fourteen hours straight, over the ocean to boot!

I often wondered where this fear of flying came from. Something about putting my life in the hands of another man, in a big machine that from all appearances only got off the ground via the grace of God, left me sweating and clutching the armrest on every takeoff, and I was uneasy even when at cruising altitude. I figured it must have something to do with growing up in an alcoholic household, where the unpredictability of my father's behavior left me feeling like I couldn't relinquish control to another man. Later in life my father sobered up, and remained so for more than twenty years, but the effects of a childhood with an alcoholic father had taken its toll. Every time I flew, it was the same. I would hear the pilot's voice come over the intercom, and the scared boy within unconsciously heard my father and imagined him in the pilot's seat.

"This is the pilot speaking." My father's rough voice would bring shivers to me. *Shut up! And sit down!* my father-pilot would command. *Listen to your flight attendant. And if you don't, I'm coming back there with the belt!* I could feel a trickle of sweat run down the inside of my arm. *Now sit back and relax, while I see if I can figure out how to get this thing off the ground!*

Flying scared me. I used to sit in the back of the plane because, statistically, that is the safest place. Later on, I realized that the farther away I sat from the pilot, the more afraid I was, because it was a control issue. Even sitting closer to the cockpit made me feel better. Best yet, if I could listen to the cockpit/ control tower communication that was sometimes available on the complimentary headsets, I could find some comfort and begin to relax.

"Only half an hour till boarding," Cathy noted out loud. "Do you think I should call the kids one more time before we take off?"

"No, don't bother," I said. "They've probably forgotten all about us and are out playing with their friends."

I wasn't just trying to comfort her. For the most part, the four boys would, no doubt, do fine without us. However, something about this trip made all of us a little nervous. Perhaps it was the knowledge of the unrest in South Africa, or the simple fact that both of their parents were going away overseas for the first time, that caused the concern I could see in their eyes as we said goodbye. Our third son, Owen, who is the most sensitive of all, teared up as we left and looked at us as if it might be the last time he'd see us in this world. Seeing his face, I had to turn away in order not to burst into tears myself. I also had a sense of foreboding. Ronnie and Jason, the two older children, were well aware of our nervousness surrounding this trip as we spoke openly of the danger and weighed all of our decisions. The only boy that I didn't think was too worried was our youngest son, Steven. At nine years old, he was one of those fearless types, and he didn't worry about anything.

Our older children also tended to worry more—a trait that I had inherited from my mother and that I unconsciously passed down to them, although it took me a long time to realize it.

I was raised with the unquestioned certainty that life is fragile and that anything can happen, any time. Like I said before, every time I got sick as a child, my mother would worry over me, pace back and forth, and take my temperature again and again. She never said anything, but her actions, and especially her face, burned a clear message into the core of my being: "Oh, no! He's going to die!" I grew up with the strong sense that I had to be as cautious as I could be or I might end up getting killed for no good reason. It was also quite possible, as my mother made plain so many times, that one day I might just up and die without doing anything at all.

I realize now that she had a good reason to think so—she had a child who did get sick and die. Her first son, Bruce, was a bouncing boy of two when one day he developed a bad case of pneumonia, and he died in the hospital within hours. She always felt that she could have prevented it somehow, if only she had taken greater precautions. I was her only other son, and by the time I came along she had convinced herself that boys were somehow weaker than girls. She feared that I too would die. She did everything conceivable to prevent this from happening.

I unconsciously adopted this same fear when it came to my own children. Whenever my first child, Ronnie, became ill and developed a fever, I would panic, check his temperature again and again, pace and worry, and say, "Oh, I think he's going to die." Cathy, on the other hand, looked at me as if I were nuts. She'd say, "He's got a temperature of 99.9. He'll be fine! Relax. They're pretty tough, you know. They don't just up and die."

No doubt, Mom wasn't responsible for all of my fears. It was later in life that I came to realize that my father suffered from alcoholism. His alcoholism had certainly contributed to this category, to the fear of what might happen next and the feeling that the world was often out of control, but I had also collected and cultivated plenty of fears on my own. Besides, my mother also taught me to survive, to work hard, and to move forward no matter what might be trying to hold me back. She passed along to me a strong German work ethic and even a well-honed sense of humor about life, which she had apparently adopted from her only brother.

So I grew up with fear, fear of not being in control, fear of the unknown, fear of death, and these fears followed me into adult life. I lived a fairly normal life, but any time I felt out of control, or when I was confronted with anything that looked remotely dangerous, whether in actuality or imagined, extreme caution took over. This often led me to hold back, and it kept not only me but also my wife and family from having more adventures or relaxing and enjoying ourselves. At the time we took this trip to South Africa I was working my way out of it, but the fear was no doubt still my biggest obstacle to overcome.

As I grew both emotionally and spiritually as a father, I realized that I had been passing that same sense that life is fragile along to my children. The real turnaround came for me at a church camp called Laurel Camp in the mountains of Pennsylvania. It was one of those camps that started in the sixties that combines camping with sharing groups, worship, good food, and a lot of cooperation. It was the first time I had ever gone to a family camp. Watching everyone's kids running around in the woods without supervision, I was convinced that one of them would end up getting killed. I especially worried about Steven, because he was fearless and often hurt himself. He was one of those kids who didn't know what danger was, and the boys would egg him into things like jumping off the roof or running after barking dogs and the like. He hurt himself so often, playing rough and rabble-rousing, that he always had bruises all over his head. Surely he would die up here in the merciless mountains of Pennsylvania!

Laurel Camp not only gave people an opportunity for building friendship and community, but was also a time to reflect on life and where you may want to make improvements and grow spiritually. At one of the sessions that year, I came to a real recognition that I had been passing along the fear of death to my kids. Not only did I want to stop putting fear into my kids, but I wanted to reverse, if possible, the damage I had already done. But how many opportunities would I get to do that? I couldn't just gather them together and say, "You know how I've been sort of scaring the hell out of you, and unconsciously telling you you're going to die?" I could imagine them with their mouths open and eyes wide, bobbing their heads in affirmation—right. "Well, I was wrong. OK?" It would never work. What I needed were opportunities, many opportunities, in conversations, in attitudes, in living life together from a new place. I prayed to God right then, perhaps one of the most sincere prayers I ever prayed. I prayed that I might have an opportunity to begin to reverse the damage I had done with my children, and as soon as possible, lest I forget.

It was not more than three hours later that Steven, the roof jumper, came to me and asked me if I would go for a walk with him in the woods. As we walked, mostly in silence, I began to reflect on the insights I had received just hours ago, and wondered whether this would not be a good time to introduce the subject of fear and safety, and how it's not necessarily that easy to die. Well, just about that time, Steven stopped along the wooded path, tugged on my shirt to get my attention, and then looked at me with the most wondrous smile on his face. He had some realization he wanted to share with me. He said, "Do you know something, Dad?"

"What's that, Son?"

"I haven't died yet."

I almost fell over when I heard those words, and tears instantly came to the surface. I took his hand, looked into his wondering eyes, and said with a confident smile, "Son, it's hard to die." I then looked up into the sky with a mischievous smile and thanked God for giving me the opportunity, whispering in amazement, "You've got to be kidding! Thanks."

Cathy roused me from my deep thoughts about our children. "It's time to board."

"OK. Let's go." It was time. I had to get on that plane and take one of the longest flights in commercial airline history. I swallowed my fear, grabbed my things, and headed for the end of the line.

3

IS THIS THE END?

We boarded the huge jetliner and found, to our surprise, that we had seats in the upper compartment of the Boeing 747. These were about forty seats up on the second floor, right behind the cockpit, and were a bit more spacious than the seats downstairs, though the same price. We settled into our seats. Cathy sat on my left, next to the window. The man on my right was a professor who had been to South Africa before, and was returning to give a series of lectures at a university there. He was American, but the upstairs cabin seemed to be filled mostly with chipper, well-to-do, white South Africans. The flight attendants, whose accent and manner revealed their South African heritage, gave a cheerful, "A pleasant afternoon to you, and welcome aboard!"

"You seem pretty relaxed," Cathy said to me as she tucked James A. Michener's fat novel about the history of South Africa under the seat in front of her.

"Well, I suppose I am." I tried to make a joke.

"I was looking for halos over the other passengers' heads and didn't see any, so I guess we're safe."

"Good. It's a long flight. I'm hoping to sleep for much of it."

Cathy, like her son Steven, seemed to have no fear of death. Her father, a rocket scientist in the early sixties, had died of a sudden heart attack when she was eight years old, but that loss didn't seem to have affected her the way that my brother's death affected our family. I envied the way she was oblivious to danger, but not her sadness. Though she worked hard and very lovingly to raise her children, and she also enjoyed her part-time job in education, she always seemed a bit restless, searching, longing for something deeper. It was clear, especially in times of marital discord, that her wounded child, the little girl within, longed for her father. Even at age thirty-eight she still called him Daddy.

Cathy was and is a beautiful woman, and that faint air of darkness and restless mixed with her natural charm gave her an intriguing magnetic quality. When we first met, that combination blew me away. She also had a moral commitment and passion that would not be crushed in this crazy and ever-changing world in which we found ourselves. That was important to me. It gave me a sense of stability and comfort.

Soon after settling into our seats we were ready to take off. I took a deep breath and held tight to the armrests as the sound of the engines swelled and the plane began to roll forward. Sensing the enormous thrust as I found myself being pulled into the seat behind me, I realized what power these huge planes had, what power they had to have, to get this mini-city off the ground. And before I could finish that thought, we were in the air and heading out over the ocean. I looked across Cathy and out the window to the fading coast and blurted out in a childlike voice, "Goodbye, America!"

As I gazed out over the blue water, I began to relax. Perhaps everything would be all right after all. These huge planes were well cared for. South African Airways was one of the best in safety. And the kids, well, the kids would be just fine. They'd probably enjoy not having us around for a while. They were staying at friends' homes. It would be two weeks of sleepovers and fun for them. We'd be back before they even missed us. As I sat back in my seat I told myself that I worried too much. *This trip will be exciting. Africa! Wow! We're going to Africa! We're going to a place most Americans only read about or see on National Geographic specials! Africa! What excitement awaits us there? What adventure?* I was growing excited about it. Only thirteen and three-quarters more hours to go! I slipped into daydreams about our destination.

A few minutes later the plane shifted speed suddenly, and a noticeable gurgling sound could be heard over the roar of the engines. I had heard a lot of noises on airplanes—the weeeeee-ing of the flaps as they were extended, the chachunk of the landing gear as it locked into place—but I had never heard a sound like this before. Cathy and I looked at each other, perplexed. Unknown to us, and not yet completely understood by the pilot, a tire had blown on takeoff. The wheel had ripped apart on the runway, and it had torn three holes into the fuselage, cutting several hydraulic systems. The plane had no power for the landing gear, no reverse thrusters to slow the plane down on landing, only partial use of flaps, and it was leaking hydraulic fluid, not to mention missing a wheel!

The pilot's voice came over the intercom. "Excuse me, ladies and gentlemen." I could sense something was wrong from the tone of his voice. There was a slight tremble, perhaps of fear, perhaps of confusion and bewilderment. He spoke professionally, but his pauses and occasional stutter gave away his unsettled state. "We will not be going to Johannesburg. I—I am sorry, but we have a problem here.... We are going to have to dump our fuel and return to JFK." Most people groaned while a few gasped. "We have 110 tons of fuel we have to, to dump. It could take up to two hours." His voice sounded even more confused and agitated. "I am not certain.... We have no hydraulics for certain systems on this plane, and we are going to have to put the landing gear down by hand. The engineer is going to investigate and we will get back to you." The passengers became very quiet at this point as the seriousness of the situation hit home.

I glanced over at Cathy in utter disbelief. This could not be happening to us, could it? Could something I feared so much actually be happening? Wasn't my fear just a big joke? Wasn't flying the safest form of transportation? Was this truly happening? I could feel my heart pick up speed, and my entire body became light. My awareness of everything was rising, my senses heightened. My body was entering a fight-or-flight state with nowhere to go. I felt helpless as I listened to the gurgling plane, watched people's eyes, paid attention to the occasional comments of the people around me, looked at my wife. At that moment the pilot came back on.

"I don't want to lie to you, folks. I am not certain what is happening, and we will be making an emergency landing. I don't want to tell you this, but we will be coming in to a parade of fire trucks and ambulances.... Don't worry. This is standard procedure."

"Standard procedure?" I said aloud. "Standard for what?" I turned to Cathy and she turned to me, and we didn't say a word, but we didn't have to. As our eyes met, the words were clear without vocalizing them. *What are we both doing on this plane? What about the kids?* In my mind's eye flashed images of each one of them, with expressions of fear and distress, expressions of gloom and fading hope as they learned of our deaths. I thought of Owen's face when we left, how he had been so worried we would not return. Maybe his fear had been some sort of premonition. I remembered my own anxiety about the flight, and wondered whether we hadn't all picked up on a foreboding of some cataclysmic ending to our world as we knew it. It was too much to even think about. But I had two excruciatingly slow hours circling out over the ocean—perhaps the last two hours of my life—with nothing to do but think.

Time seemed to stop as thoughts of my children mingled with prayers for our safety. I found comfort in repeating, "For thine is the kingdom, the power, and the glory." I tried other phrases from the Bible, but for some reason this was the one that helped the most. I just repeated it over and over again in my mind, like a mantra, as I tried to control my fear. I wanted to talk about our predicament with Cathy. That's how I process things: I talk. But when I looked over at her I saw right away that she had introverted. That's how she processes things: she goes in. I tried to talk, but she waved me off. I knew why. She had enough difficulty with her own fear and couldn't handle mine.

Two hours is a long time to remain in a state of utter terror. The heightened awareness, the thoughts of my children, of the plane suddenly rolling over and plunging into the ocean, of the dark possibility of our imminent deaths, and the unbearable fear burned me out. I don't remember much of those two hours except for the fear. It was the same fear I felt when, as a little boy, I was raced to hospital wheezing and gasping for breath from a bad case of pneumonia. It was the same fear I felt as I ran from the ghosts and the cold, empty places in our house as a child, as I blocked the closet doors in my bedroom so that the monsters couldn't come out. It was a familiar feeling, but in this circumstance it was the familiar feeling at two thousand times the intensity.

My thoughts raced through one horrible scenario after another as I listened to the gurgling sound coming from somewhere on the plane's bleeding body. What would my boys do? If we died here on this plane they would be abandoned forever. No one would be there to give them the love that only Cathy and I could. No one would be able to take the time and the patience to engage them from the depth of caring, to mentor them. They would be forsaken. What a horror! What a horror to be called out of school, gathered into some room with your brothers, and to be told that your parents won't be coming home, that they have crashed into the ocean and are gone! I could see their faces change from that innocent sense of safety and comfort to terror, and then to grief. I knew that this grief would last for a lifetime. I didn't want to do that to them. I didn't want to leave them. I didn't want to die now. My mother had always said that this was a dangerous world and that we could be taken out at any moment. My God, I had thought she was wrong. All those years of worry, of fear, of caution so that nothing would happen to me, all those years added up to this moment of catastrophe. She was right all along. Those you love can be taken from you without a moment's notice. The world is a place of fear, pain, death, abandonment. Any moment now, my last vision of the kids would be shaken with the sound of passengers' screams and the breaking of plastic, steel, bones, and bodies as we plunged into the depths of the dark sea.

"This is your captain speaking." His voice jolted me out of my morose thoughts and brought an even greater sense of dread, not knowing whether he had more bad news to tell us. "We're going to go in now. The flight attendants will instruct you about what to do." As the flight attendants pointed out the exits, showed us the crash position, busily checked that all items were safely secured, and all this with a professional smile, I felt the plane make a sharp turn and begin to descend.

"Here we go," I said to Cathy in an upbeat voice, but my heart was definitely lodged in my throat. The descent back over land and to the airport seemed to take forever, and as we approached I kept thinking that the breaths I was taking might very well be my last. What an unusual circumstance, to be aware that you may be breathing your last! I managed to crack a smile, in a twisted sort of way, as I told myself that in a few moments we might all be charred meat on the runway.

We descended to what I would guess was about three thousand feet and then we just held there. We held and we held, and again Cathy and I looked at each other. Without saying a word, we again shared a thought: *He can't get this thing down!* It was at that moment that I decided to say my final prayers to God. I prayed that we'd land safely, but if we didn't, I prayed that God would look after our children in a special way, and that they would all get over the pain of our loss, and eventually get on with their lives. I ended the prayer with a special request, revealing my state of bravery, or the lack thereof: "And God, if we are all going to die, I don't want to hear all the screaming and experience the plane smashing into the ground and the burning and all that. Please God, if I have to die, can you spare me that? Can you just make it so that it appears that everything went fine and that we landed safely, and then have an angel come up to me and tell me that I'm dead? Can we do it that way? Thanks, God. Amen."

As my prayer ended, suddenly the plane dropped with incredible speed. I instinctively went into the crash position, as many did, and I remember the seat in front of me just flopping over as I pressed against it. Apparently there is some switch in emergencies that allows the seats to flop like that. I saw the couple in front of us huddled on the floor, shaking. I felt one with them. Suddenly, like a pancake, the plane hit the ground flatly, bounced hard, landed again, and rolled down the runway.

Cheers went up from the passengers. I almost passed out as an unbelievable wave of relief went through me. I yelled, "Yessssss!" and raised my hands into the air, as many of us did. As we glided down the runway, and the people continued to cheer, I noticed that the pilot applied no reverse thrusters. We were still hauling across the concrete. As the people continued to cheer I called out in a cheerful voice, "Yes! But we're not stopping!" The crowd hushed. I was so happy to be on the ground that I didn't really care what happened next. I know it doesn't make any sense, but I didn't mind if I was killed horizontally; I just didn't want to be killed vertically! The plane glided smoothly without those reverse thrusters, and the flashing red lights from the fire trucks and ambulances lit up the inside of the plane as if it were some sort of amusement park thrill ride. The lights and sirens ushered us in on both sides of the entire runway as we came to a very gradual and peaceful stop. As we stopped I laid back in my seat and sighed with relief.

Before the passengers could even move, the pilot came back on the intercom and ordered, "Nobody move! They're checking us for fire. Be prepared to evacuate. The flight attendants will open the door if necessary." I looked behind me to the nearest exit, and there was one of the attendants, all smiles, with his hand firmly grasping the emergency handle. I didn't care. I knew if we had to evacuate, we'd be fine. It was over! And we had made it!

It turned out we didn't have to evacuate, but the plane was unable to taxi back to the terminal under its own power. It had to be towed, and this process took another hour and a half. As we sat on the plane the pilot tried to entertain us by calling attention to the "beautiful New York skyline" and other points of interest that now, under the circumstances, seemed completely irrelevant. As I sat there I remembered my prayer to God, and so I turned to Cathy and told her my little deal.

"So if I am dead now, an angel is supposed to tell me I am dead. Cathy, am I dead?"

Cathy smiled mischievously and beckoned me to come closer. She put her mouth to my ear and let out the loudest belch I had ever heard.

"Yes! I'm alive!" I exclaimed. "I am alive!"

4

AFTERSHOCK

By the time the airlines had safely towed the plane to the terminal, booked all 240 of us into local hotels, and bused us to those hotels, it was close to midnight. They told us to check back in the morning, as they would be fixing the plane overnight for a new attempt at overseas flight tomorrow. I didn't even want to think about getting back on that broken plane. As I entered the hotel room I was shaking from all the tension and excitement. I had so much energy from the ordeal I didn't know what to do with it. I called friends of ours who I remembered had experienced an emergency landing a few years ago. I knew they would empathize with us about our fearful experience. It was good to talk with them. They were glad to share their ordeal and listen to the story about ours. I also called my parents to tell them what had happened. My father, as usual, seemed disinterested and aloof. He was more curious about how quickly they could fix something like that and get the plane up and running again.

My mother took the exact opposite approach. She took it all to heart, and in her charming, worrisome way, basically warned me not to get back on the plane.

When we finally settled down into the hotel bed, I had a hard time getting to sleep. In fact, it was one of the worst nights of my life. My entire being had overloaded from the tension. I laid there, body and mind buzzing away like an electric razor dropped and abandoned on a tile floor—turning, churning, vibrating, whirring, humming, growing hotter and hotter, buzzing and buzzing. At the same time, I longed for sleep, being completely exhausted from the stress. It was hell. I kept flashing back to sitting in my seat, listening to the gurgling sound of the plane, gazing at the other passengers, at Cathy, out the window at the ocean below, worrying about the children, and praying. The shock of it all was too much. This, mingled with the relief of surviving such an ordeal, and the jolt of energy such relief brings, launched me into another world. It penetrated and shook my very being.

I don't know when I finally fell asleep, but I remember waking up just at dawn, crying out in terror. "It's coming! It's coming!"

Cathy woke up and tried to make sense of my cry. "What? Grant, wake up."

"It's not locked in there anymore! It's coming for me! Ahhhh!" I cowered like a little boy in terror. Finally, after a moment of reorientation, I realized I had been dreaming. It was a dream that brought terror and the memory of something I had put behind me. But apparently, the shock of the emergency on the airplane had brought it to the surface again.

"Oh, man! I'm sorry. What a dream! It was about the ghost in the New Room."

"The ghost in the New Room? You're kidding. What about it?"

"I dreamed it was set free. It no longer had to stay there, and it was coming for me."

"Whoa! That's wild."

"Yeah. It was like I was a kid again, and relived the whole thing. Isn't that crazy? I guess this is my unconscious response to yesterday."

"That would make sense."

"I suppose so. It *would* make sense. I almost died in there when I was a kid. And, I don't know... That ghost. I never did figure out what was happening in that room, but it tied into my childhood fears about the unknown and death. Yesterday certainly brought back that core fear—facing the unknown of what would happen on that plane, the real possibility we might just die!"

We sat on the hotel bed and chatted about the dream and the ghost in the New Room. "I don't know what it is about you, Grant, but you've always seemed to be aware of those paranormal things much more than me. It's like they follow you around or something," she joked.

"Well that's a comforting statement!" I said with surprise and a bit of sarcasm. "There was nothing as weird as this ghost in the New Room. I don't remember anything else happening."

"What about the CD player?" she replied.

"Oh, well, that wasn't the ghost. That was God. Anyway, that happened in Chicago."

What Cathy was referring to was the only other really paranormal incident I had experienced. But I hadn't connected it to the ghost in the New Room, and at the time I doubted they were related. There was a time a few years earlier when I was really down about my life because of some circumstances at work, and I was listening to music as a way of cheering myself up. I loved the soundtrack of the movie *The Mission*, especially song number five on the CD. It has a very beautiful and comforting melody. In a quiet and contemplative frame of mind, I walked over to the CD player with the *Mission* soundtrack CD in my hand. I gently pushed the on button. Not only did the player turn on, but the CD tray opened to receive my CD. The tray isn't supposed to open on its own. It opens when one presses the eject button. But big deal! I was only mildly impressed. As I placed the CD onto the tray I said, "Thank you. Now, play number five for me." The CD player closed as I hit the eject button, and before I could punch any more buttons, bingo! Number five lit up on the machine and started playing. I was a bit startled, and I smiled. In my state of despair I just saw it as God's little way of saying, "Hey, I'm here. I'll take care of you." I laughed at his little stunt and said, "Thank you. I suppose I needed that." The ghost in the New Room? Eight hundred miles away? Maybe. For the more scientific minded, some sort of remarkably empathetic "electrical short in the CD player."

All of this taken into account, I did feel I had a strong connection to the spiritual world. Often I felt answers would come to me either by some inner, barely perceptible voice or by a dream. These things seemed natural enough, but they were not particularly pleasant experiences.

Since much of my childhood in that house seemed so dark and gloomy, even scary, I spent most of my childhood and early youth running from my fears. I left the house often to explore the outside world, building forts in the woods with friends, camping out, smoking, and later drinking. In fact, the drinking did a good job of numbing the fear and emptiness, and it shut down most of the psychic ability as well. Thank goodness I grew out of that habit at the time, but another one took its place. As I became an adult I immersed myself in work, trying to be successful, focused on making the grade. Anything was better than turning around to face the stillness and the darkness that always seemed to stand behind me, the ghosts that Cathy said seemed to follow me everywhere I went. The dream of the ghost in the New Room, now free to come after me, touched a deep fear. It touched the frightened child within me. What did it mean? What could be happening?

After our conversation, Cathy and I just did what we always did after an unexplainable incident surrounding that particular room—we shrugged our shoulders and moved on. The ghost in the New Room never did make any sense. It never added up to anything. It just remained an oddity to me. After having that dream, the memory of the ghost was fresh, and the fear of the unknown that surrounded it welled up within me. But I saw no purpose in it. It was just one bad dream following the nightmare of the plane ride the day before. I was full of fear. The one question that bothered me the most had nothing to do with the dream. Sometime later that day, I had to get back on that same plane. I wondered if I could do it.

The plane to South Africa didn't take off for another seven hours. In the meantime I gained courage by spending time in the hotel lobby, looking for and hanging around the many pilots who happened to be spending the night there on layover. I didn't talk to them. I just sort of snuck up on them, hovered near them, hoping to hear some of their calm conversation about an upcoming flight, hoping some of their cool courage would rub off on me. Just before we left the hotel to return to the airport, I called a therapist friend and asked him to talk me back on the plane. He did. He said, "Do you have any sleeping pills? Take one now. See if it helps." I did, and it did help. Right before boarding the pilot told everyone in detail what had gone wrong the day before. He assured us that everything was right now, and that he would certainly not attempt a flight unless everything was working properly. Groggy from the sleeping pill and satisfied with the pilot's explanation, I boarded the plane.

Not too many moments later we took off for South Africa. I would love to report that we arrived without incident, but the truth—one we didn't learn until later on—is that the plane blew another tire on this takeoff as well. However, since nothing else broke apart as a result of this, we continued our flight to South Africa minus one tire.

PART 2

AFRICAN AWAKENINGS

5

SURVIVORS

Our plane touched down on the runway in Johannesburg with a hard thump. It was the nicest thump I had ever experienced. After fourteen hours in the air, I was glad to be on the ground again. We made it!

We were picked up at the airport by ministers from one of the more affluent white congregations and driven several hours to the coastal town of Durban. The first thing that struck me was the incredible beauty of the countryside. Stunning vistas, lush vegetation, majestic mountains, and sparkling rivers surrounded us on our journey. It was a magical land. Gazing upon it I realized the true meaning of the word "breathtaking."

The opulence of the whites there was conspicuous. Large, gorgeous homes were built into the verdant countryside. Villas and mansions dotted the coastline. Beauty and wealth abounded everywhere. But this was white South Africa. I would soon learn firsthand that it was very different in the black townships.

South Africa was a land of contrasts and contradictions. The beauty and wealth of the countryside estates was countered by the ghastly sea of makeshift huts and burning fires in the shantytowns of Soweto and elsewhere. When I first saw this, it too took my breath away, but for the opposite reasons. Another contrast could be found in the people themselves. They were the warmest, nicest, most fun-loving people Cathy and I had ever met. This was true for both the whites and the blacks we would come to know on our journey. But at the same time, a horrible monster roamed the landscape unseen. Utter disregard for human life, cruelty, and a vicious, inhuman violence lurked in the shadows there, ready to strike out at any moment. We heard story after story of killings, torture, fear, and hatred. Everyone had an experience of escaping the grip of evil, either from the old, now-fallen government of Apartheid, from the riots, or from the crime that now ran rampant throughout the land. This reached a surreal level when we sat virtually every night with the locals in front of the television, in either the black or the white districts, and watched what they called the Truth Commission proceedings. After Apartheid ended, people were encouraged to come forward during a grace period and confess before a panel and all the country the crimes they committed during the struggle between the old government and the people. If they didn't come forward they could be prosecuted later on. Night after night both black and white people, many of them prominent members of the new government, stood before the cameras and told gruesome stories of their participation in kidnappings, torture, and killings. Though it seemed to be a relief to the people watching to finally be hearing the truth, with some it seemed to spark the flame of hatred, and it heightened the tension between the whites and blacks to such an extent that I wondered whether the whole country might erupt into open warfare.

Cathy and I spent the first week with a white congregation in Durban. Their hospitality and warmth was beyond compare. Cathy and I both got along well with these South Africans. They seemed like kindred spirits. They were lively, open-hearted, and loved to have a good time. Every evening we were there they made dinner and threw a party for us at a different home. It was as if they realized how precious and how fleeting life can be, and they were going to enjoy themselves while they could. Coming off of our emergency landing at JFK, I was ready to enjoy life a little bit more—and thankful that I had life to enjoy.

In our conversations, the men and women spoke of their love for South Africa and their hopes for new changes now that Apartheid was over. They spoke nobly of the country's effort to rebuild toward a greater equality and opportunity for all. They were ready to dig in and tough it out. At the same time, their fear of their current circumstances—the loss of white control, the growing chaos, the wildly rising crime and violence—was manifest. Most of the homes in the white sections of South Africa were beautiful and well kept, but also had become mini-fortresses. Bars covered every door and window. Many homes, especially near the black townships, had walls with razor wire crowning the top for extra security. Each home was equipped with a panic button so that if the residents were attacked, they could call in paid armed security nearby. They spoke each day of their fear and the flight of the whites from their country.

After already being burned out by our emergency landing and shaken by the dream I had, it didn't take much for me to catch their fear. Everywhere I went, I did so with a sense of heightened awareness that was not so different from what I had experienced on the crippled airplane. Every time we were taken somewhere in the car, I had a reminder of the danger as the driver asked us if we had our fake wallets on us, and if our real wallet and passport were safely stowed away on our bodies.

I hadn't kept something hidden in my pants like that since I used to smoke cigarettes as a kid. It was unnerving. I also kept remembering the one pastor's words about carjacking and how they wouldn't let the women go, but would do terrible things to them. I was more than nervous, and I prayed daily for courage. This was before even entering the segregated townships, where we would be in the most danger of all.

About a week passed of wonderful visits, entertainment, meals, meetings, and classes that I ran for the local people there. We were coming up on the weekend when we would be driven into Claremont, the nearest black township, to preach to two of our black congregations gathered at a single church there. The night before, one of the members of the white congregation took me aside with a strong look of concern on his face. "Sorry old boy, but you should know. You're doing something very dangerous going in there tomorrow. Most of us have never been in there. I'm just telling you straight up. I don't want to be responsible for you going in there without having your eyes open." He was seriously concerned.

Even though I did have fears about the trip, I told him that I felt I had to go there to support the local ministers and congregations who had to live with their unfortunate circumstances every day of the year. Besides, the ministers there were excited about me coming. I wouldn't disappoint them for the world.

These ministers, who were of Zulu origin, remembered that a few years earlier I had bucked the system of church politics and started a fellowship of priests dedicated to fighting the good fight against ignorance and evil. It was called the New Church Military, or NCM for short. It was a fellowship of support. This idea sprung out of my own sense of discouragement and loneliness in this work. Not only was it difficult trying to interest people in forming a new relationship with God and starting a new life, but it seemed that the greatest enemy to my own well-being and what I was trying to accomplish were my own personal demons. These fears and doubts about my abilities or what God could do in my ministry tried to stop me practically every day from reaching out to others. I thought to myself, *If I feel this alone and discouraged, I bet others do as well.* I decided to go all out in forming a new fellowship in support of this struggle to do the Lord's work. I made up an initiation ceremony similar to some African and also Native American rituals. Ministers who joined pledged to fight the good fight, and I gave each a set of dog tags to remind them that they were not struggling alone. After their initiation, I sent them regular communications from others who were in similar circumstances through my office. I'd also send out little gifts occasionally, such as special little homemade posters with inspirational quotes, or even short little audiotapes with a collection of inspirational music. One of these tapes that the African ministers particularly liked was a mixture of music from two movie soundtracks—*The Mission* and *Henry V.* The song "Non Nobis Domine," sung by Henry's men after their miraculous victory over the French, served these ministers well in reminding them that even in their difficult circumstances, against such great odds, miracles can happen.

I had been informed by at least one of these particular Zulu ministers that they viewed their inauguration into the NCM as the first real acceptance of the black ministers among the brotherhood of the white ministers. Whether or not this was coincidental to other factors, such as the fall of Apartheid, it was clear that they felt gratitude to the NCM for this recognition and acceptance. They saw me as a type of spiritual warrior, and they were looking forward to welcoming me with open arms to their country.

Now, as a scared kid from the suburbs of Philadelphia about to enter their territory, I felt less than noble. But I wouldn't miss visiting them for anything. Cathy and I were both ready and excited to see our fellow laborers in this particular vineyard on the other side of the world.

We drove into the township the next morning with probably the only couple in South Africa who did not worry about the danger around them. The Reverend Jefferson Stipe and his wife, Helen, two Americans, were working in retirement in South Africa in a church supervisory role. They were the type of people who you just knew had some sort of force field around them. They drove wherever they wanted, any time they wanted, never worried or took precautions about the dangers, and nothing ever happened to them.

As we drove into the township Jefferson announced with a huge smile, "Hey, listen up. This intersection is very famous! Look around. More cars are hijacked from this intersection than any other in the country."

"Cool," I joked. "Why don't you pull over so we can take some pictures?" He slowed down. "OK, OK ... Keep driving!"

The ride to our destination was not long. We barely entered the township, and, though the houses were in poor condition, it wasn't as bad as I expected. I wondered why the whites didn't come here. It didn't look that bad. As we pulled up to the church building, I felt fairly relaxed. Members of the Zulu congregation came running out to meet me. I smiled and felt relieved, even rejuvenated. They led Cathy and me to the church building. I walked into the vestry and there before me were the two local pastors—men I hadn't seen in over a year, since they visited the United States. Mablevi Buthelezi and Albert Mtanna, Africans in their late fifties, both stood robed for the service. Mablevi was proudly wearing the dog tags I had given him on the outside of his robe—something he apparently did every Sunday service. Both men were grinning from ear to ear as they strolled over to greet me with a handshake and a hug.

"Good to see you, maaan! Graaant! You look good, maaan. We heard about your ordeal on the plane. So sorry. Shame, maaan." I loved their accent and the tone of their voices. It carried so much feeling in it, so much love. I relaxed completely, looking forward to leading the worship service with them. About seventy-five people were already gathered at the church. The church was a very modest two-room building with what looked like clay walls and a tin roof. A few open windows allowed light to enter into the sanctuary, and the people sat on bare wooden benches facing an old table with an open copy of the Bible resting on top of it. I would be giving the service, and the two local ministers were going to take turns translating my talk into Zulu for the people.

Just before the service started I remembered that I needed a prop for my talk. I wanted to do the story of Moses raising his rod in the air as Israel gained victory over the Amalekites. However, I didn't have a rod with me. I thought that perhaps I could find a stick or something like it hanging around the property. I looked across the vestry and spied a black ornamental stick with a knob on it protruding out of a paper bag. I looked at the two ministers with wide eyes and a smile, pointed to the rod in the bag and said, "I need this. Can I use this?"

"You need this?" They looked at each other with disbelief. "You need this? It is a miracle!" they exclaimed. Apparently, they had bought this rod as a gift for me. It was called a knobkerrie, a traditional weapon of the Zulu nation. They had planned to present it to me as a gift after the service. They laughed heartily that I had picked it out and asked for it. They kept looking at each other and muttering, "It is a true miracle." They agreed that I could use it during the worship service, but they still wanted to present it to me in front of the congregation afterward. I said that would be fine. I was just thankful to have the stick for a prop, miracle or not. We walked into the sanctuary to begin the service, the traditional weapon in my hand.

The service was beautiful. I had never heard such wonderful, spontaneous harmonies, and Mablevi and Albert dynamically translated my words into their language. I felt the people were with me the whole way. When I came to the part about Moses holding up his rod in his hand I held up the knobkerrie with both hands and spoke of the power of truth in a person's life. As I held up the knobkerrie I noticed a charge go through the congregation. Some yelled in excitement. Some looked nervously out the window. Some smiled ear to ear. I raised the rod again and called out, "The power of the truth." They cheered in return and even more of them sat up in their seats and looked out the windows excitedly. I had no idea what was going on but it seemed to be working like a charm.

After the service the members of the congregation provided a small banquet for all of us. It was a variety of African dishes, fried chicken, fruit, and "cool drinks," which are various fruit and soft drinks. It was at this time that we had a wonderful talk with the two Zulu-born ministers and the people of the congregation. They spoke of their hardships during the time of Apartheid, and also what it was like to live in these townships. Albert, who was pastor of one of the local congregations in Kwa-Mashu, told of the time he refused to let a local terrorist group meet at the church. They blew out the windows that night with a bomb. Mablevi spoke of the riots and the killings. In a way, it was hard to imagine that these terrible things had happened, because these people seemed so peaceful, loving, and in many ways content with their lot. I felt for them deeply, and I marveled at their cheerful disposition. I asked them about this. They replied, "Ah, yes. The Africans are special people. The vast majority of Africans are loving and forgiving people, and more than this, they are survivors!"

"Survivors," I repeated. "Man, I can relate to that." I was

thinking of our ordeal on the airplane. But even more than this, that word—survivor—was resonating with me on a cellular level. It fit in somehow with the ghost in the New Room, the running from the darkness, the life I had carved for myself despite the fears. I felt a sense of brotherhood with these men through this notion of survival, though my circumstances didn't compare to the challenges they had overcome. I became acutely aware of this difference when Mablevi hushed the crowd and presented the gift of the knobkerrie to me. The two of us stood before the people as he spoke. What he said stunned me.

"Friends, I would like to explain this gift to Grant. This is a knobkerrie. It is a Zulu traditional weapon. It is like your sword. It is a symbol of the truth, of the war against evil and oppression. It is a symbol of the struggle each one of us faces to make something of our lives and to follow God's ways. Members of this congregation, we are giving this traditional weapon to this man, because this man is a warrior!" He reached out to give it to me, and the people began to applaud. I almost fell over. Me, a warrior? Guilt rushed over me as I thought of myself cowering in the airplane, as I thought of the fear I had coming to this place. Then I glanced over at Mablevi and remembered that not more than a year earlier he had lost his son here on these streets. Thugs had killed his son on the way home from choir practice. I thought of my own sons. I wouldn't be able to go on if anything happened to one of them. Both Mablevi and Albert, their families, and all of their people had seen so much horror, had experienced so much pain and loss. They had lost loved ones and had their churches bombed. Many had been beaten by government soldiers, starved by the lack of provisions, and trapped in poverty. They had struggled just to make ends meet and stay alive. They were the true warriors. They were the heroes. I felt more like a coward in their presence.

Tears entered my eyes as I thought of Mablevi's son and the

irony of him giving me the honors. But I accepted the gift with courtesy and dignity, not for me, but for them. They needed a hero. They needed to know and believe that someone out there in the greater world, beyond these invisible walls of prejudice and injustice, was fighting for what was good and true. They couldn't honor themselves for their own struggle and survival, but they could honor others for their struggles, and in so honoring others, feel comfort in their own accomplishments. It seemed to me to be a beautiful illustration of Jesus's words that if you give to others it will be given back to you. I took the knobkerrie and shook Mablevi's hand, and the people applauded once again.

Later that afternoon, as members of the congregation began to wander back to their homes, I had a chance to talk alone with Mablevi. I told him of my fear during the flight, and how I was nervous coming into the township. I said, "Mablevi, I don't deserve this knobkerrie. I'm basically a coward. What battles do I face? You are the ones facing the real battles. It's life and death out here."

He turned to me with an almost disturbed look. "I know what you are trying to say, Grant. But you are in error, maaan. The battle to stay alive is important. However, the bigger battle is the one that goes unseen. The real battle is the one taking place right now all over the world, between what is right and wrong, good and evil. I may face so much earthly strife, but it is the spiritual strife which *causes* this earthly strife. Grant, in helping us with our spiritual struggles, you lead the battle on this higher level. In simply supporting me and the others against the power of hell, against the fear, the inertia, the evil that would stop us from living, you are helping us fight the only really noble battle. The knobkerrie is yours. Whether you are a coward or not, you are here. You are here, maaan! Thank you for coming here." He reached out and shook my hand. I felt a little better, and I accepted his words with a nod and a smile. Coward or not, it was important for me to accept this traditional weapon. It was important for Mablevi and the others, and perhaps it would become important for me in gaining the strength I needed to fight the battle against the fears that held me hostage inside. Though I didn't quite understand why he had given me this gift fit for a warrior, I was touched. I would never forget his words of honor or his face. The knobkerrie sits over my fireplace even now, as a reminder of the good fight—or, as he called it, "the only noble battle."

When we returned to our host in the white district that evening, I excitedly spoke of the day's events and how moved I was by the service. On the television I noticed that a huge rally had taken place in the center of Durban, and that hundreds of Zulus were carrying knobkerries in the streets as they marched. I said, "Oh, look at that. They're carrying knobkerries. Mablevi and Albert gave me one of them. I used it in the talk. It was really something. Every time I held the thing up in the air the people got all excited and started shouting and looking out the window."

"You held up a knobkerrie?" my host asked in a mildly alarmed voice. "You see those people marching in the street? The knobkerrie is the Zulu symbol of freedom. It's been banned by the government from public display. They're carrying it in defiance of the government. Grant, you could have been arrested. And in this country, they just throw away the key."

I had to laugh as I thought of myself raising that knobkerrie and shouting, "The power of the truth!" No wonder these people shouted and looked excited. Here was this white guy from America risking his life and liberty for the cause of freedom. Wow! And he didn't even know it. I smiled and replied to my host, "Maaan, didn't you know. I'm a warrior!"

6

TRAUMA

After more than a week in South Africa, Cathy had already called and spoken to our children several times. She was missing them badly, as any mother would, but she sensed from her brief conversations with the boys that they were doing just fine in their host homes. I also missed our boys, and eagerly looked forward to seeing them once again. I knew that our return home was only a week away, after we visited the congregations in Johannesburg and Soweto.

I was beginning to enjoy myself, especially visiting people and sightseeing. A few days before leaving Durban for Johannesburg and Soweto, we were gallivanting all over with our friends and tour guides, Jeff and Helen Stipe. We frequented some great restaurants, walked through beautiful parks, and even swam in the Indian Ocean. Although I still kept an eye out for potential danger, it was beginning to feel like a vacation. I needed that.

It was on our last day in Durban, during lunch

at one of those idyllic restaurants with Jeff and Helen, that I suddenly became ill. It felt as if I had been hit by a train. I turned white and started to perspire. A wave of nausea came over me, then aches and chills all over my body. I almost fell out of my chair as I began to fade in and out of consciousness.

Cathy and the others noticed immediately that something was wrong. They wondered if it was something I'd eaten, but I had hardly touched the meal in front of me. It wasn't the food. My entire body was reacting, not just my stomach. I felt like I was going to die. I told them I thought I'd better lie down. They helped me into the car and drove me to the home where we were staying. I could do nothing except crawl into bed and shiver there.

I lay in bed for a couple of hours. Cathy came and checked on me periodically, and I kept saying to her, "I don't know what's wrong with me. I've never felt like this before in my life. I don't understand it."

"Should we cancel the dinner tonight?" she asked. I had forgotten that we were supposed to go for a very important dinner at a couple's house in less than an hour. This particular couple, Linda and Mark Smith, were the parents of a good friend and colleague of ours in the States. They had been trying to have us over all week, and were really looking forward to seeing us.

"I'm not sure. I don't think I should go, but this may be our only chance of seeing them. Damn! Why did I have to get sick now?"

Cathy called them and explained the situation, telling them our plans might have to change. It was something of a surprise that Linda insisted we come anyhow. "Oh, Mark and I know all sorts of special remedies for these things. If Grant is going to be sick, he should be sick over here. We can help him. Please come. We'll come get you." Linda and Mark were both dabblers in New Age healing, and also avid believers in homeopathy. They insisted that they would be able to "fix me up" if I came.

Cathy explained to me that they had insisted and, with a bit of a concern on her face, asked, "Well, what do you think?"

"Let's go," I replied. "But I won't be able to eat." I did sense I was gradually beginning to feel a bit better. The chills had gone away, and I only felt a little achy and a bit queasy. Mark drove over, picked us up, and took us to his house. It was only three minutes away by car. Soon I was sitting on their couch with a homeopathic remedy in my hands. Mark and Linda sat down with us, and we began to talk about their life in South Africa, about their family, and about their plans for the future. After about twenty minutes of conversation the phone rang. Linda answered it.

"Yes. Yes. She is right here." Linda looked disturbed as she handed the phone to Cathy. As Cathy took it I somehow knew it was not a good phone call. Something had gone terribly wrong. I stood up and went to stand next to her.

"Hello? Yes. Yes. What happened?"

My heart stuck in my throat. Cathy's face was turning pale.

"I don't understand.... Yes? Where is he now?" she asked the anonymous voice on the other side of the phone call. I knew it was someone from home, and I knew it had to do with one of our boys.

"Who?" I whispered.

"Is he conscious? Which hospital?"

With those words, I sank back down on the couch. The little energy I had left drained from me instantly. Something awful had happened.

"It's Steven, Grant." Cathy broke off the telephone conversation to tell me. "He's been hit by a bus." She began to cry. I grabbed the phone.

"Hello? Who's this?"

"This is Mike." It was the father of the family Steven was staying with. He was a doctor, so he would know exactly what was going on. "There's been an accident. It looks like things are going to be OK. Steven was hit by a bus. He's conscious now and the doctors are fairly optimistic."

"Where is he? What happened?" I heard his words, but they weren't sinking in. Mike explained that Steven had been trying to cross the Pike, a very busy road on the way to school, in a place where there was no crossing guard. He ran out and was hit by a bus—SEPTA, Philadelphia's public transit system—and was thrown forty-eight feet. He had been delirious when the ambulance picked him up, and in and out of consciousness at the hospital.

The shock of hearing that our littlest son had been hit by a bus, and that they didn't know yet how serious his injuries were or if he would walk again, was enough of a blow to absorb as parents. Being on the other side of the world when we received the news was torture.

Cathy was crying. "I just want to be there with my baby," she repeated. "I need to see him." I could only try to console her. I too felt the fear and frustration. We remained on the phone for several hours with various people, including immediate family, doctors, ministers, and friends, many of whom were at the hospital. The parents who were caring for Steven were wonderful in conveying exactly what was happening as it happened. However, Cathy and I both felt we needed some sort of verification of what was going on from someone in the family. Were things really going well, or was it wishful thinking? I asked if my parents were there. When I was told that they were, I asked to speak to my mother. I knew she would give me the straight story. If anyone would be worried—even terrified—that the worst would happen, it would be Mom. If she thought things were really OK, then I knew I could begin to relax a little.

"Hello?" My mother sounded like the receptionist at a government agency. Her voice was cold, businesslike, tight. It was really tight.

"Mom?"

"Yes?" It took me a moment to realize why her voice was so strained. How difficult this must be for both her and my father! They were probably reliving the terrible ordeal when Bruce died. I began to understand. I felt like I had to bring it up. I was afraid to hurt Mom, but it was obvious that this accident was putting her through hell.

"Mom, this must be hard for you."

"I don't ..." She paused. "It's very hard. But of course we wouldn't be anywhere else right now!"

"Mom, level with me. How does he look? Is he really going to be OK? Tell me the truth."

"Well, Grant, they *say* he is going to be fine. He doesn't look very good, but they *say* he is going to be fine. I don't know what else to tell you. All the tests are coming back hopeful." She kept repeating that they *said* he would be fine, emphasizing the word *said* with her typical worried skepticism. However, I knew she wasn't going to lie to me with comforting words when she felt no comfort. She would never underestimate the danger.

Over the course of the evening the reports of Steven's condition became better and better. No broken bones. No apparent damage to the brain or spine. Only a concussion so far, and some scrapes and bruises. The good news made us relax a little. Finally, one of the hospital doctors got on the phone. "This kid is extremely lucky. He must have had an angel with him. I have never heard of a kid being hit like that, flying so far, and not even breaking a bone. It's a miracle. It's a true miracle." He put Steven on the phone for us, probably thinking that this would be a comfort to Cathy, but it turned out to be just the opposite.

"Hello?" Steven's voice quivered, barely audible.

"Steven, this is Mom and Dad. Are you feeling OK?"

"Noooooooo. I feel awful . . ." He broke out in tears, which caused Cathy to do the same.

"Steven, I wish I could be there with you," Cathy sobbed. "I'll make sure someone stays there with you. I'll see you just as soon as I can."

We took turns talking to Steven and then each one of the other children. Jason and Owen learned of the accident when they were taken aside by a teacher at Bryn Athyn Elementary School and told very gently about Steven's condition. They seemed to be handling it all fairly well. But Ronnie, our fifteen-year-old, wasn't taking it as well, and for a very sad reason.

"Dad, I wish you were here. Dad. I thought he was dead. I thought he was dead, Dad."

"What happened?"

"When I got to school we could hear the sirens. There were even two news helicopters out over the Pike. Some guys in my class came in and said that a boy had been killed." He paused and sniffled. "They wanted to go out and see the blood. . . . I thought, 'Man, that poor family, to lose a boy like that!' Then the teacher came in, and he didn't know what people were saying. He just came up to me and put his arm around me and said, 'Ronnie, that boy was your brother.' I thought he was dead, Dad!" He cried a bit and then regained his composure. "They took me in another room and kept giving me these reports, like they said he was awake in the ambulance, and then that he didn't break any bones. I thought this was odd and wondered how he died. Then they asked if I wanted to see him. I was like, 'What?' They said he was awake and doing fine, and I couldn't believe it." He laughed a bit and sniffled. "Man, I wish you guys were here."

Both of us wished we were there too. Cathy was already planning to cut her trip short and try to catch a plane home the next day. No matter what, it would take approximately two days for her to get there.

Before we ended the hours of phone conversation with the hospital, the doctors said that they wanted to keep Steven at least overnight for observation. We certainly wanted someone to stay with him, and we thought perhaps Fay, the mother of the family he was staying with, would spend the night. If not Fay, then maybe my mother or Cathy's mother. But when we asked, they responded that my *father* was going to stay! I found that impossible to fathom. Dad? Shut-up-and-go-to-sleep Dad? I couldn't believe it. I asked for my mother.

"Mom, why don't you stay? Why would Dad stay?"

"He wants to stay, Grant. He insists on it."

"Won't he fall asleep? Why would he want to stay? I don't get it."

"Of course he won't fall asleep." She was a bit perturbed by my questions—or maybe it was the tone of my voice, as if I didn't believe her or didn't trust that he'd be able to care for Steven the way that Mom had cared for me in dangerous times. "Do you want to talk to him?"

I put the phone to my chest and told Cathy that it was for real. She grabbed the phone.

"Hello? Hi, Dad. Are you going to stay with Steven tonight? Uh-huh. OK." She handed the phone back to me.

"Hello, Dad?"

"What?" He was agitated, most likely because he picked up on my hesitation.

"Are you going to stay there?"

"Yes!"

"Are you going to stay up all night?"

"Of course. I'm going to sit here by him all night. What's the problem?"

"Are you sure?"

"Yes. I am going to sit here all night. I promise. I won't go to sleep or even leave the room." He was serious.

"Is that OK, honey?" I turned to Cathy, and we both sort of shrugged our shoulders and agreed that he would stay.

"OK, Dad. Thanks. Call us first thing in the morning."

"OK. Bye."

"Bye."

Before returning home that evening, Mark Smith called South African Airways and arranged for Cathy to be on the next flight to the United States. We would have to fly to Johannesburg first, and there she could catch a late-night plane home. After much discussion, I decided to stay in South Africa. I would cut the trip short, lopping off the safari they had planned for me after my official business was completed. I just wouldn't have enjoyed myself knowing I could be home with my son. However, I could still visit the two congregations in Johannesburg and Soweto, meet with the ministers there, and preach in Soweto. The people in Soweto especially were counting on me being there. I didn't want to let them down. After that, I would return home.

The next morning Cathy and I reflected on what had happened the night before. We were still in shock. We both realized as we spoke about it that I had become violently ill at what seemed to be the exact time, according to what everyone had told us, Steven had been hit by the bus. It was strange to think that it might have been sympathetic pains halfway across the world, but it was too much of a coincidence to be anything else.

Cathy busily packed her things. As much as she might have been enjoying herself in South Africa, she was already home in her heart. She cried off and on that morning. In fact, she cried off and on all the way home until her son was in her arms again. Even then she cried some.

As we packed, my mother called to update us about Steven's condition. "He's with us now," she said. Her voice was much more relaxed than it had been the night before. "He wanted to stay with us until Cathy gets home." Hearing her calm voice brought me even more relief. I reflected once again how hard this incident must have been for Mom and Dad, and though I didn't want to hurt her any more by bringing it up, I knew it was on her mind.

"Are you really OK? What was that like for you? Was it tough on you?"

"It was very tough." That's all she said. She didn't want go into details. I didn't want to push her, but something inside of me needed to know more. I didn't know what that was about, but I continued to ask her about it. "Did it remind you of Bruce?"

"Yes. It was very hard for both of us." That is all she would say. I let her off the hook.

"Well, you sound a lot better now."

"Well, Steven is OK. That certainly helps. . . . It will be nice when Cathy gets here."

Before closing the conversation I just had to ask one more time about Dad. "Mom, why did Dad want to stay at the hospital? It doesn't make any sense to me." I just wondered why he, of all people, wanted to stay.

She grew quiet. I could tell that she was moved. Something I said had touched something deep. I thought about withdrawing the question, but then she spoke.

"When we took Bruce to the hospital, they told us he was going to be OK, and that we should go home." Her voice went silent for what seemed a very long time before she continued. "And so we went home. . . . And then they called us and told us that he had died." She paused, and I could hear her swallow hard. "Your father wasn't going to let that happen again. He wouldn't leave this time. And this time, the boy lived!"

It was the most she had said about Bruce in many years. It seemed this terrible episode, though painful, was the beginning of much-needed healing for Mom and Dad. Cathy and I shared their relief.

"The boy lived!" My mother's words rang in my ears like church bells. "Thank God!"

7

HOKA HEY!

Twelve hours later, Cathy and I were embracing and saying goodbye in the international terminal of Johannesburg's airport. Getting Cathy on a plane back to America wasn't as easy as we thought. When we checked our luggage in Durban, Cathy was informed that she was not actually scheduled to fly out that evening and that the plane was booked. We told our story. Cathy cried. I begged. Nothing. They told us to check in at the counter in Johannesburg. Maybe they could help us. Cathy cried the entire flight to Johannesburg. People kept looking over at her with concern. I explained the story of our little boy, and why she was crying. "Shame. Oh, shame!" they replied. This is the South African way of saying, "I feel for you."

When we arrived at the airport counter the people there still insisted that she couldn't get on a plane to the US for at least a few days. Finally, out of frustration, Cathy called one of our hosts back in Durban, Sharon Dobbs, just to cry about it with someone. Sharon told Cathy to stay by the phone while she made a few calls. Sharon called back in ten minutes and told Cathy to go to the counter again. A ticket had been reserved for her. Apparently Sharon asked to talk to the duty controller, who is the boss of who flies where. It happened to be a woman, and a mother at that. Sharon talked mother to mother, and the duty controller felt for our situation and made the necessary arrangements. When Cathy and I returned to the counter, their attitude had changed completely, and they gave Cathy a ticket to leave that evening.

Cathy and I held each other in the airport like newlyweds parting company for the first time. "Have a safe trip," I told her. "Call me when you get home. I don't care what time it is. And give Steven and all the kids a big hug and kiss for me, and tell them I'll be home soon."

"OK. Listen, you're going into Soweto. Don't do anything stupid. Promise?"

"Me? Relax, Cathy. I'm too scared to do anything stupid."

Cathy gave me another hug and then disappeared down the corridor to the plane that was waiting for her. I wondered to myself if I would ever see her or my children again. I really didn't know. Eight days earlier I would have laughed at the notion. But now, after the recent shock of Steven's brush with death and our own close call on the airplane, I was so shaken that I felt anything could happen. Any of us could be taken out instantly. I felt like I was in a movie. I did not know what would happen next, but the way things were developing, I was sure it would be dramatic. I was just hoping this drama would end as a comedy rather than the tragedy I feared.

I spent the next day and a half in Johannesburg with the Reverend Anders Tate and his very Caucasian congregation, though he was one of the first to invite local black Africans to join them after Apartheid ended. Anders and I went to theological school together, and it was wonderful to become reacquainted with him. He and his wife, Jessica, showed a lot of caring and concern for what we had been through. In fact, when I met with the congregation, they all wanted to know how Steven was progressing, and how Cathy had taken it, and how I was. They listened and responded, "Shame, shame!" Then they wanted to know what had happened on the plane the week before. It had been in the papers there, and they wanted a personal account. It also turned out that one of the members of the congregation in Johannesburg lived next door to the pilot. Small world! He had told her about the tire popping on the second flight as well.

Anders and Jessica had three adorable little children—a girl and two boys. Jessica confessed that she worried about her children a lot. It was hard for her not to, with the rising crime and instability. I asked if they ever thought about leaving South Africa.

"We have thought about it. A lot of people have left," Jessica replied.

Anders added, "But it's a dilemma. How could I leave my own homeland? I wouldn't want to leave our congregation here without a pastor. We are hoping things will progressively get better."

"If it really starts falling apart, we'll leave. But we're ready to tough it out," said Jessica.

"How do you live with the tension? I suppose you just get used to it," I ventured.

"Oh, no, Grant. You never get used to it. Not just the adults, but most of the kids, for instance, are in therapy on a regular basis trying to cope with the stress. They've all heard of or know someone who has been killed, carjacked, or robbed at gunpoint. It's not something you ever get used to," replied Anders.

I understood his point. I knew that I wouldn't be able to

cope in such a precarious situation. I had to hand it to them for their bravery in deciding to stay in South Africa. As we sat in their living room and talked and watched their children play on the floor in front of us, I took time to observe each child, each grin and giggle, their innocence and delight in their games. I smiled at this, but also wondered, in my fragile state of mind, what terrible nightmares they would suffer when they grew older. What darkness would they be running from? I felt for them, and I said a silent little prayer for each of them.

That night as I prepared for bed I thought about the adventure to come. Tomorrow I would go into Soweto. I had asked Anders if he had ever been there, and he said yes, he had traveled to Soweto a number of times. But he confessed that he was among the very small minority of white men to go into that place. He told me it would be "a bit of a shock" when first entering the township. "It's a very different site," he said. He also told me honestly that there was a real danger in going into Soweto, but that Kosan, the Zulu minister who would be driving me in, and whose home I would be staying in, knew the terrain well. "He'll keep you out of harm's way," Anders assured me.

Part of me was terrified, and this brought me shame. Before getting into bed, I knelt down beside the bed with my face pressed into the covers and prayed. *Dear God, I need you to give me courage. I don't ask to be more courageous, because I don't have any courage left in me. I need it to be a gift, gratis. It's all gotta come from you, God. Please give me courage. Anything I had has been drained out of me in the last few days. I'm ashamed of myself. I'm ashamed. Please help me.* I knelt in silence for some time.

Rising from my prayers, I had a realization. Though part of me was very fearful, another part was now determined to see the mission through, to rid myself of the fear and do the job. I stood up, opened my suitcase, and pulled out an outfit for the next morning: an old but trim army shirt and some green pants that reminded me of army fatigues. If I was going in there, I would be going to battle—against my own fears and doubts. This outfit I had chosen was my soldier's uniform for the day.

I thought of my sons and how much I missed them and wanted to see them again. But I also thought of how proud they could be of their father. Not many dads got the opportunity to venture into Soweto and help the people there fight against the darkness. I quietly whispered the Native American war cry I had taught my sons: "Hoka hey!" It was a way of saying, "Everything is in God's hands." When the Sioux chief Crazy Horse led his warriors in battle, he shouted, "Hoka hey! It's a good day to die." *Hoka hey* literally means, "Let's roll!" He was exhorting his warrior to move forward, because this is a good day to give it all, even your lives. That saying inspires me to move forward and to give myself into God's hands, regardless of the circumstances—part of my process to heal from my fears.

I longed to be with my sons again, sitting in front of an evening fire, talking about life's secrets, the earth and the sky, ancient warriors, sacred ceremonies, and legends. Truly not knowing if I would see them again, I had to let the thought of them go. Turning my thoughts to the real battle before me, I gave myself into God's hands. "Hoka hey," I repeated to myself with a smile. Pride and excitement gently rose within me. "It's a good day to die!"

The next afternoon Kosan Masubo and his wife, Sarah, drove up in their little four-door sedan to take me to their home in Soweto. Kosan was a tall, slim black minister in his early sixties who looked a lot like Nelson Mandela, the famous president of South Africa. In fact, occasionally people mistook him for Mandela. Sarah was a lot younger than Kosan, and a very kind, thoughtful, and effervescent woman. We embraced with smiles and a warm exchange of greetings. "Shame about your boy, Grant. Is he truly all right? It sounds like a miracle," Kosan said.

"Shame Cathy couldn't be with you. I had prepared so many things for her. I hope she is feeling better about your son," added Sarah.

"She's on her way home right now," I told Sarah. "She should be there sometime tonight. I know how much she wanted to visit with you, Sarah. She's very sorry she couldn't come."

"Shame! Well, tell her we love her, and that we understand completely why she went home. Here, now, you sit up front so you can have a full view of Soweto. We're taking you to the center of Soweto! We want you to see everything!" Sarah spoke with pride, and also a trusting sense that I would understand and sympathize with their situation. I knew that I would. But to hear we were going to the "center of Soweto" caused my heart to beat a little faster. As I sat in the front seat and buckled my seat belt, I could feel my body begin to tighten up and, just as on the airplane, my sensory awareness heightened. The time had come to enter Soweto!

Anders's warning that driving into Soweto would be "a bit of a shock" turned out to be the understatement of the year. Crossing over a bridge, we left the world of opulence and abundance, of refinement and grace, and entered into a world left behind—or rather, forced to remain behind. We left contemporary Western civilization and entered the Third World. In this case, it was a world neglected, the dumping ground for the modern metropolis and, practically speaking, the recent social and economic prison for hundreds of thousands of black Africans. Here and there new construction revealed the change in governmental policy and the beginning of the modernization of the black townships formed by Apartheid. But a new building here or a modest set of modern row houses there were offset by seas of makeshift huts formed out of cardboard, tin, and pieces of fiberglass. There were areas where these shantytowns sprawled out as far as my eye could see, with thousands living virtually on top of each other in the dirt, refuse, and open sewage. The smoke of the fires burning outside many of the huts caused a reddish haze to hover over the place, giving it an otherworldly look—like a lost refugee camp on Mars. It took my breath away. Kosan slowed the car down to allow me the time to take pictures, while Sarah explained to me that this was something not many white men have seen.

As we drove down the dirt street, I saw fires burning everywhere, burned-out buildings, abandoned cars, and men in uniform on some street corners with rifles in their hands. There were masses of people, chickens, goats, and occasional oxen roaming the streets. Practically everyone we passed stopped, looked, and pointed at us in surprise, at the white man in the car with the black man. I began to get nervous.

Sensing this, Kosan said, "Grant, you see these people? Most of them think nothing ill about you. Yes, some look at you and hate you. Some think because you are white that you are rich, and they would like your money. But most, Grant, most fear you. What you see in their eyes is fear from years of abuse."

I nodded, understanding what he was trying to convey to me. But I couldn't stop thinking about those who hated me, and kept silently repeating my warrior-mantra, *Hoka hey. Hoka hey. It's a good day to die.*

After about forty minutes of driving through the streets of Soweto, we came to a stop in front of a modest home with a wall around it and an old wooden gate. As we stopped, people on the streets gathered around the car to see me. I grabbed the handle to open the door and Kosan said, sternly and abruptly, "Don't get out!" It sounded an awful lot like the pilot's voice the week before when he commanded, "Nobody move!" I stayed in my seat as he honked the horn until a young boy came out and opened the gate. We drove into the tiny compound and he shut the gate behind us and bolted it.

"Welcome to the heart of Soweto! This is Simeon and Simosihle's house," Kosan announced with pride. Simeon and Simosihle Tsibolali were another New Church minister and wife who lived and pastored a congregation here. "Simeon lives almost in the dead center of Soweto," he explained. "We are taking you, the Tsibolalis, and some others out to dinner in celebration of your being here." I again nodded and smiled. Kosan told me to wait in the car while he and Sarah went in to see if they were ready. A few minutes passed, and then Kosan came out and beckoned me to come into the house.

As I opened the car door and walked toward the house, I could hear familiar music playing inside. I entered the door and was greeted by Simosihle, who welcomed me with a warm handshake and ushered me into the living room, where the music was playing. As I walked in I saw both Kosan and Simeon sitting like two schoolboys in front of an old audio cassette player, eyes twinkling with joy and bright smiles on their faces as they sang along with the song that was playing. It was the cassette tape I had sent them, and the song was "Non Nobis Domine"! When I saw their joyful faces and realized that they were singing this song of hope and bravery in my honor, I teared up. The contrast between my fear and their joy, and the overflowing sense of love surrounding me as they sang, brought up too much emotion for me to contain. When they saw my tears, they both instantly teared up too. Simeon said softly, "Oh, Grant! Oh, Grant! It's so good to see you, maaan. It's so good to see you." As the song ended Simosihle handed tissues to each of us, and we sat there in silence for what must have been at least six or seven minutes. Then other family members joined us, and we ate some cheese, drank some "cool drinks," and took photos of one another in various group shots. Almost instantly I felt very much at home.

Later that evening we all piled into a van, picked up a few

more people, and headed back out of Soweto to a very fine restaurant in downtown Johannesburg. We talked and laughed on our journey and Sarah, poking me with a smile, remarked, "I see you are a lot more talkative going out of Soweto than coming in." People laughed heartily and then listened for my response.

"That's true," I said with a chuckle, "And that's because it's now night and people can't see that I am a white man!" The car filled with a burst of common laughter.

"Yes, but wait until we reach the restaurant in Johannesburg. There, we will be the ones who feel the eyes," remarked Sarah. People eagerly nodded in agreement. I wasn't sure what she meant until we were seated at our tables and began to be served by our white attendants.

I had spent a few summers in my youth working in the American Deep South. I remembered witnessing some of the prejudice, which was slow to dissipate despite the advances that came with the civil rights movement. In that restaurant I felt I was in the Deep South once again, but perhaps during the height of tension, when blacks were first entering what used to be forbidden white territories. Here in South Africa, only a few years earlier the blacks would not have been allowed in this restaurant as patrons. To have whites actually serve blacks in this setting was unheard of. I could sense the tension when the waiter took orders. On several occasions, some of the whites stood nearby and mumbled to each other what sounded like racial slurs about our group and sneered and smirked at us. They did not want to be serving these people.

Kosan and the others took it well and even played it up a little, which made me nervous. One of the little girls who was with us had received the wrong drink order. When the girl's mother demanded it be exchanged without charge the waiter fell quickly into a rage. He called the manager, and all three began to yell at each other. As voices raised and fingers pointed, the white men's faces became beet-red from anger, as if they were going to explode. Sarah stood up and said in a firm, calming voice, "Sirs! Sirs! Please! Please, sirs!" The two men quieted down, but they looked over at me as if to say, "What the hell are you doing here?" I smirked back at them. The manager suddenly smiled. He said, "Yes, madam," disappeared into the kitchen, and returned with a fresh drink for the girl. Everyone settled down and the altercation was over. I didn't know exactly what had transpired to calm things down, but I was glad that it had ended.

As we wrapped up the meal and it came time to pay the bill, I pulled out my wallet to offer to pay, but Kosan and the others insisted that this was their treat. It was their way of thanking me for coming. I realized that this cost them a small fortune, and expressed my deepest gratitude as we left the restaurant. On the way out the door I was the last to pass the waiter, another table hand, and the manager, who were standing in a line at the door, poised for something. The manager sneered at me as I opened the door. "Kafir-lover!" he blurted out in a semi-hushed tone. I smiled and walked out. I did not know exactly what that meant, but I had a pretty good idea.

When we drove back into Soweto it was getting quite late. Several people had to be dropped off in different parts of the township before we could go to Kosan and Sarah's home. We dropped their two daughters off at their home first, and then Kosan asked me if I minded accompanying him and Sarah on a short "midnight tour." There were a few more places he wanted to show me. I said, "It's OK with me." This prompted some discussion among those remaining in the car about how wise this would be, considering the danger at this time of night, but Kosan, in his gentle way, insisted. As we drove off into the night, Sarah turned to me with a delightful grin and announced, "You are now doing something that we don't even do because of the danger! You are getting a tour of Soweto after midnight!"

I grinned back at her. At that point I had basically run out of fear, and turned whatever I had left over to God, at least for the moment. We drove around for close to an hour. I saw more burned-out buildings, abandoned cars, gangs, police, and so many little campfires lighting up the night.

As we pulled into the modest but very well-kept development where I would be staying, and pulled in front of the garage at the Masubos' home, a gang of young men stood near the house. Once again I went for the door handle, and Kosan told me to stay in the car. Kosan got out and opened the garage door. He drove into the garage unseen by the young men, shut the garage door, and said that it was now safe for me to exit the car. I grabbed my suitcase and headed inside the home.

The small but immaculate home included a kitchen, living room, several bedrooms, and a bath. It was very nice, and not what I expected for a home in the township. In some ways things were getting better for the people, though very slowly. Kosan and Sarah had worked hard to get this home. He was a superintendent for several schools in Soweto, and she was a certified nurse. Together they were able to live in one of the better areas of the township, with neighbors who took pride in what they had. They looked out for each other as well.

When we walked into the living room, one of the girls we had dropped off at the house before our tour informed me that Cathy had called from the United States. She was back at home and everything was fine. "But she was a bit concerned," the girl said, "because I told her you were out touring Soweto. She said, 'He's doing what? Isn't it after midnight there? I told him not to do anything stupid!'" We all laughed, but then agreed I better call her immediately. I did, and Cathy and I talked for about ten minutes. I explained my adventures and told her that everything was fine. She, in turn, told me all about being reunited with little Steven. He had a few cuts, bruises, and scrapes, but, all things considered, was in good shape. Before Cathy hung up she said, "You promised me not to do anything stupid and then you went and did something stupid! Please don't do that again!" I promised, and we said goodbye.

I went to sleep on a magnificent bed with lace coverings, special pillows, and a few neatly arranged stuffed animals. Sarah explained that she had prepared the bed for Cathy, and was so sad Cathy could not sleep in it, but that I should enjoy it. As I fell onto the bed and rested my head next to the window, I could see the glow of the fires burning in the shantytowns just a few hundred yards away. The smell of the wood burning brought comfort to me. There were no bars on these windows, no razor wire, no alarms. This was Soweto, South Africa! I fell asleep quickly and had the best sleep of all my nights in this foreign country.

8

RUN INTO THE ROAR

The rest of the time in Soweto went very quickly. I preached to two congregations at Kosan's little church that Sunday, which was the last full day I would stay in Soweto, and the day before returning briefly to Johannesburg and then flying home. About 140 men, women, and children sang glorious African hymns, clapped hands, shouted, praised the Lord, and enjoyed the celebration of life and of God. Again I used the knobkerrie as a visual aid in my sermon, feeling that it would deliver a message of hope. At the same time, I wanted to prove to myself that I was, in some way, not the coward I had made myself out to be. It felt good to raise that stick in the name of God. It felt even better to see the delight on the variety of faces in the congregation.

After church we feasted together, sang, and even danced to a few local folk songs. Their dancing exemplified their passion for life. They were joyfully celebrating simply being alive. It taught me that people can be happy even in the most difficult circumstances. I saw more clearly than ever that we could all do a better job at helping to alleviate burdens, to free all from oppression, to relieve pain where it can be relieved. I had the sense that this was the noble battle Mablevi Buthelezi had spoken of. But at the same time, I understood from what I saw in the townships of South Africa that the human spirit is strong, very strong, and can not only adapt and survive adversity but flourish despite it. In the chaos and inhumanity that seemed to exist all around, especially in this place, I still felt a real sense of hope for the human race, for the loving survivors.

That night, my last night in Soweto and my last night in South Africa, Kosan made a pitcher of iced tea and pulled out some crackers, and we sat on the couch in his living room to talk. We talked about his hopes for his little school and for the church. We talked about what it was like to be a minister, and how we ended up in this field. We talked about the history of South Africa. We also talked about deeper, more personal subjects. Kosan spoke from love, wisdom, and tender care. He was like the wise and loving grandfather everyone wishes they had. I wanted to hear more from him, especially about his courage, which was so very much part of his character. I knew that anything he shared with me about facing his fears and challenges would help me face mine.

"You grew up here in Soweto, didn't you?"

"Yes. And not too far from here, either. I have seen things, Grant, you would not believe. There were riots just down the street from here. So many people! It was like a sea of people. And then the soldiers came and started shooting. It was terrible, maaan."

"How did you cope? How did you survive in such fear? I mean, I grew up in a lovely little town outside of Philadelphia. I never saw anything really bad happen in my life, except perhaps on television. I was never threatened, never felt that I was in danger or that I would be harmed, and I have a lot of fear. Tons of fear, Kosan! How did you do it? How did you survive?"

"Grant, first of all, we all have fear. There isn't a person on this planet that doesn't fear something, and most people fear many things. We all have fears no matter our circumstances. A rich man, for instance, has much, but because he does, he may fear he will lose what he has. A poor man may fear he will go to prison if he does not pay his bills. A mother fears for her children, and a child may fear he will not be fed. We all fear something. So, do not be too hard on yourself because you have fear. It is what you do with that fear. It is how you react to it that makes all the difference."

"And what do you do with it? How did you survive?"

"Well, survival may have had more to do with God's providence mixed with a bit of luck. Who knows who survives and why? But I will tell you, maaan, the way I coped with the circumstances was not to run away from what I feared. Imagine if we had run away from our fears in this country, where would we be now? We would still be under the rule of Apartheid. Imagine if the white men who ruled this country had not faced their fears and allowed Apartheid to die. I tell you, maaan, more massacres would be happening on these streets even now. You must face your fear. That is the African way.

"There is a story that has been popularized in your country, but it has its origin here in Africa. It is about facing your fear. It helped me, and I know it will help you. When lions go on a hunt, the old and tired lions have the loudest roar, but they are too weak to chase the antelope. In fact, the antelope are fast creatures. They are so fast that even the youngest and swiftest lions could not catch them. So how do the lions eat? The old and weak lions hide in the tall grass. The young lions find a herd of antelope and try to chase them toward the tall grass where the older lions are waiting. As the antelope approach the grass, the old lions give out a thunderous roar. When the antelope hear it, they stop in their tracks and turn to run toward the younger lions, who easily attack them and kill them. If the antelope had continued to run into the roar of the old lions, perhaps some would have been killed. But many more would have lived, and it is not inconceivable that all of them would have escaped unharmed, because the old lions are weak and slow. What this teaches is that you must keep going, maaan. You must run into the roar. If you run into your fears and face them, you will escape their sharp teeth and terror. You must run into the roar of the old lions."

I listened intently. What he said made sense to me. But how could I face my own fear when I didn't even know what it was truly about? "I suppose since my little airplane adventure and Steven's accident, I'm finding it hard to get back on my feet. Have you ever had anything like that happen?" I wanted some sympathy, or at least another good lesson, from Kosan.

"Oh, Grant, which story do you want to hear? I'll tell you the closest I came to death. I mean, I thought I was dead, and somehow I escaped, through the grace of God almighty. When the African National Congress was fighting against the government they asked if they could secretly meet at our three schools. I did have a quarrel with the ANC and its use of violence against violence. That approach never helped anyone. But I was more concerned for the schools. We had all worked so hard to start the schools and receive permission from the government and all. If we had allowed the ANC to secretly meet there and then if the government found out, they would have brought the heavy equipment in, maaan, and leveled the buildings. What good would that be? As superintendent of the schools I told the ANC that they could not meet there.

"Well, one night they all gathered outside the school, right after a meeting I was attending. There were crowds of people and they brought me outside and accused me of being a spy for the government. Now, do you know what they did to the spies, Grant? They burned them! They locked them in their cars, turned the cars over, hit the petrol tanks, and set them on fire. Many were executed that way. As my accusers shouted that I was a spy, the people grabbed me and put me in my car. I saw the clubs in their hands. They surrounded the car and I could feel it lifting off the ground. I thought I was a dead man. I knew it was over for me. I just prayed to God and made my peace. Then, out of nowhere, and for whatever reason I do not know to this day, the very man who was accusing me, who was the number-two leader at the time, suddenly shouted to the people to stop. He told them to let me go, that I was not a spy. He ordered another man to jump in the car with me and drive me to the top of the hill and let me go."

"What happened? Where did you go?"

"I drove home," Kosan answered smartly. "It was a miracle! But I tell you, I built that church and school you saw today not more than fifty yards away from where this happened. And today the only gatherings there are the children getting ready for church! Do you understand, Grant?"

I understood and was grateful for the stories. They were hitting home. It was like medicine for my mind and emotional well-being to hear of his predicaments and the courage with which he faced them. We talked for quite a while, late into the night. His wisdom seemed so basic and yet so profound, so tender and yet so deep. It was healing to me. I wanted to ask him about one more subject before going to bed. He had spoken of facing fears, of overcoming times of trial and of crisis, of escaping death itself. This gave me a sense that I would heal from the latest circumstances thrust upon me. But I still wondered about the deeper fears, about the shadows and the ghosts of childhood that I knew I was running from.

"Kosan, do you believe in ghosts?" I asked during a pause in the conversation.

"Why?" he joked. "Have you seen one lately?"

"Well, not lately, but when I was a child it seemed we had one hanging around the house. It was more of a presence than anything else. I know that may sound strange ..."

"No, that is not strange at all," Kosan answered abruptly. "One of the things that attracted me to join the church we both pastor now is the teaching about the reality of the spiritual world. I was particularly impressed with Swedenborg's book *Heaven and Hell.* It contains the most complete picture of that world that I have ever found. Wouldn't you agree? There is only a thin line that separates those who have passed over to the other side and those who remain. Africans believe strongly in the spiritual world and in spirits. We are all spirits, though we here on earth have not yet shed our earthly bodies."

"Yes, but what about ghosts? Spirits hanging around here and all that? Do Africans believe in that kind of thing?"

"The answer to your question, Grant, is that we not only believe in spirits, but we often see spirits. The African is much more in tune with spirits than the white man. This is true of your American Indians as well. They are very much more aware of the spirits who are with us at all times. We are connected to them and they to us, because, as I said, we too are spirits in earthly bodies. I know you have studied the American Indian. Remember when you tried to get me into one of their sweat lodges?" He chuckled. "You know of their belief in the spirit world. It is the same with the African, or even more so."

I had studied Native American religion. I was especially interested in their rituals, such as the sweat lodge Kosan had mentioned. This went well beyond the moderately conservative church that I served as a minister, whose ritual was about as traditional as a Christian church could be. In fact, I received a lot of grief from some church members for experimenting with another culture's ritual. But the sweat lodge did something for me that I couldn't get elsewhere. It was alive, moving, and a bonding experience for me and my family.

The sweat lodge was basically a primitive sauna with a prayer ceremony. Native Americans would heat up rocks, bring them into an enclosed tent or lodge, and pour water on the rocks while taking turns in prayer. I had learned this ceremony from a former childhood friend, John Finley, who had since become a bona fide tracker. A tracker is someone who has been trained to follow the trails of different animals and even humans. Much of this training is taken from ancient Native American culture and tradition. In his training, John had not only been taught how to develop and use the skills of the Native Americans, but also learned of their spiritual practices. John had been taught the sweat lodge ceremony as part of his training, and he shared it with me. I was so impressed with it that my boys and I, with some friends, built a lodge in our backyard. We'd sweat and pray together practically every other week. Back in the late eighties, during the Men's Movement, it was sort of a "guy thing," with fire, dirt, sweat, and so on. It was a wonderful and very spiritual bonding experience for all of us.

I was aware that spirits played an important part in Native American religion. They called those warriors who had gone before "the elders" or "grandfathers." These spirits were said to be present to give strength in the sweat lodge. Native Americans believed that people and spirits were very connected. Coming from my Christian background, we never called on the spirits, because that seemed like ancestor worship or something bordering on Spiritualism. I had enough trouble with ghosts hanging around in my childhood to risk awakening some more. But we did honor those who had gone before, and because of the power of the sweat lodge, I clearly understood what Kosan meant when he said that the Native American belief in spirits was similar to the African belief.

"Grant, you asked me if ghosts are spirits who have somehow not left the earth," Kosan continued. "I think most of the spirits who are with us are there for a purpose. Many are guides. They are, as you say in your culture, our guardian angels. But there are other spirits who seem bound to the earth for one reason or another. Something holds them here, and they must be set free."

"I suppose you mean the popular idea that ghosts are spirits who are stuck here on earth trying to work something out. You know, the old movies where the medium comes in and tells the ghost, 'You can go on now! It's OK. Your problem is solved!' That kind of thing?" His explanation had sounded a bit too Hollywood to me, and I wondered if Kosan had seen the same movies.

"Well, sometimes that is the case. But often times it is not that the spirit needs to work something out. It is that the spirit needs us here on earth to work something out before that spirit can move on. Perhaps they are not all here of their own accord. Perhaps it is we who don't let them go. Sometimes we can hold on to them without even knowing it."

"Well, I'm not holding on to anyone. That idea gives me the creeps," I responded with a shudder.

"If you really feel you have met a ghost, and that ghost is haunting you, it may be that you are not holding on to *someone.* But perhaps you are holding on to some *thing*—some idea, notion, memory, way of thinking. And that *something* is haunting you *and* your ghost," Kosan replied.

"What do you mean?" I asked, puzzled.

"Like I said, it is a fine line that separates our worlds, Grant. We are all connected, related, bound together, especially those we love and those who love us. These bonds do not necessarily dissipate with death. We often think of those who have passed on as the ones doing the haunting. Who is to say that we here, with all our troubles, illusions, fears, and desperations, with all we refuse to let go of, who is to say that we are not the ones who do the real haunting? Perhaps we are the ghosts, the cold shadows, the breath of frigid air that passes in the night. Perhaps we are the ones who haunt those in the spirit world."

"Do you believe that?" I asked in amazement.

Kosan paused, smiled, glanced up in the air and back toward me, and said, "I don't know. But it certainly sounds good!" We both broke into a belly laugh for a few moments.

It was an intriguing idea, and it certainly sounded like it had some truth to it. We are the ghosts, or perhaps we are the ones who are haunting them! So many of the ghost stories I had heard, or even the ones I had experienced firsthand, seemed to revolve around living people's attempt to rectify their own lives or settle their own memories. The guilt-ridden ghosts who walk the hallways at night in gloom and shame may do so because we refuse to let go of their stories. Because we don't let the memory of their deeds pass on, perhaps we sentence them to walk the earth, unable to let go until we let go. The active and even violent poltergeist may reflect the camouflaged strife in a family or even concealed abuse of one type or another, or perhaps simply a youth's own struggle with his or her electrically charged yearnings, or the explosive longing to simply be an adult and be free. Were we the real ghosts? Did we haunt the spirit world by holding loved ones back from passing on to their final abode, like thoughts and memories we wouldn't let pass from consciousness? It was an intriguing idea.

9

I CAN'T BELIEVE THIS
IS HAPPENING!

❦

Crossing the bridge from Soweto back into the suburbs of Johannesburg, I found myself once again surrounded by lush green landscapes and opulent homes. However, after staying in Soweto, my view of South Africa had changed forever. The poverty and violence of the townships had been a shock to me, and I felt deeply for the people there. But rather than becoming jaded, I found hope. The Africans were survivors, as Mablevi Buthelezi had said. They were bright, wonderful people. Experiencing both sides of South Africa, getting to truly know the people, I felt a strong sense of respect and even admiration toward them. South Africans were incredibly brave people, the blacks for what they had endured, and the whites for what they chose to endure by eliminating Apartheid. What I had learned is that evil does not have to beget evil. The human spirit is strong. When bad things happen to us, certainly we can experience much pain, grief, and discouragement. But we are not sentenced to a life of these. Our inner spirit, though beaten and bruised, can survive. In the long run, that spirit can flourish. We can continue to hold our heads high and, like the Zulus, raise our own personal knob-kerrie with pride.

We do not have to become paralyzed by our fears as we look to an uncertain future. Inaction born from fear can cause more destruction than taking steps toward change. The story of the lions and the antelope had a profound effect on me. It seemed to me that even though South Africa stood on the brink of cha-os and crime was out of control, what the people had chosen to do was to run into the roar. They made a decision to abandon the old way of fear and its particular brand of law and order in search of true justice and humanity. Having plotted this course, the lions were now chasing. I hoped and I prayed that peace and order would rule and that South Africa as a nation would es-cape the lions. These noble people deserved nothing less.

As we pulled into the airport at Johannesburg, I smiled, realizing that soon I wouldn't have to carry a dummy wallet anymore or maintain that extra sense of vigilance and aware-ness. Soon I'd be on the plane heading home! I wasn't going to be killed in Africa after all! That was almost a surprise to me. The whole sense of foreboding had been for nothing, I sup-posed, except perhaps as a premonition of those two seemingly close brushes with death. But everything had worked out just fine, almost as if nothing ever really happened. That fact in it-self was strange to me. I experienced so much stress with both emergencies, and both ended up being of no physical or life-changing consequence at all. I was very glad for this, but since the experiences were so anticlimactic, as it were, I found it hard, nearly impossible, to release the anxiety. It just stayed bottled up inside. No real conclusion: no real release. Something inside me told me that I desperately needed to grieve, but since everything had worked out so well, I could find nothing concrete to grieve about. Something inside, perhaps the voice of my son Steven or my own child within, whispered sadly and desperately, "Cry! Please! Cry for me!" In Africa, I was too much on guard, too vigilant, too caught up in my "good soldier" attitude to grieve for anything. I knew that perhaps when I returned home, got off the plane safely, and held Steven in my arms once again, then I could let go and cry. I longed for that time.

As I opened the door to exit Kosan's car, I could hear the whining of the jet engines on the tarmac nearby. The instant tightness in the pit of my stomach reminded me that though I was leaving crime-ridden South Africa, I still had to face the long flight home. It was an eighteen-hour flight with a quick refuel on a tiny island in the Atlantic called Il de Sol. I was nervous about this, but I quickly reminded myself, as I had so many times before, that I was safer in that plane than in the car I now occupied; statistically, I was safer in that plane than I was in my own house. That fact had always brought me some comfort, but with all the craziness I had been through, I couldn't shake the sense that something was about to go wrong. *One step at a time,* I told myself. The first step was leaving the country. *Concentrate on that first. Then you can worry about the plane if you want to.* Allowing myself to entertain one fear at a time may not have been the most healthy approach to my growing neurosis, but it did stop me from being overwhelmed with the fears I was experiencing.

I said goodbye to Kosan and Sarah at the airport entrance. We hugged and laughed. Kosan and Sarah loved life so much and celebrated it at every moment. It was such an honor to get to know them and become their friend. They told me to give Cathy a hug for them, and also to hug little Steven. "We've been praying for him, you know. He must be a special boy, with special angels," Kosan said as he handed me my suitcase. I smiled, waved to this darling couple who had cared so well for me, and looked out over the African horizon one last time. "Goodbye! God bless!"

I walked into the airport, checked my luggage, and got my boarding pass. In this particular airport, all passengers wait in a lounge until their plane is announced. I sat down and watched the large television screen. I had seen only a little television in Soweto, though most of the nicer homes in Soweto have televisions. I found it sort of ironic that some of the poorest people in the world have televisions, and even more ironic that these same people don't see the best of television, but rather the trash. What came on from America were mostly the old cop shows and sitcoms that didn't make it in the United States.

However, this time as I looked up at the television screen, I saw familiar faces from CNN. I couldn't hear very well with all the racket in the airport lounge, but apparently something bad had happened, and this was a special report. They were showing pictures of a dark lagoon and pieces of debris. I asked a young, well-dressed man next to me if he knew what happened.

"A plane crash in the US. Shame! Value Jet. Never heard of them before. Is that a big name in America?"

"No. They're a small airline."

"Well, apparently it just fell out of the sky. They suspect there was fire on board. Shame." He picked up his suitcase and headed off as they announced the next flight.

As I looked up at the screen and saw the diagrams, the look of desperation on family members' faces, and the dark and oily water where the plane went down, I felt dizzy and chilled.

Don't go there, Grant! I begged myself. That's what Cathy would say. I tried to stop myself from thinking about the crash, but wasn't very successful. *Fire on the plane. Those poor people. What that must have been like! What would they do if there was fire on our plane, in the middle of the Atlantic?* A damp chill seemed to envelop me.

Don't go there, Grant! I tried to shut down the fear talk, but the same thought kept returning. *I can't get on that plane. I can't get on that plane.*

Well, what are you going to do, stay here in South Africa? the more rational part of me responded. *You have to get on that plane. You have no choice.*

It was about that time that they called our flight number. It was time to go to a second waiting area, where we would board the flight. I grabbed my briefcase and headed toward the door. I thought that maybe if I kept moving the fear would diminish. As I walked into this new area I realized it was a lot nicer than the first lounge. There were several restaurants, bars, and shops. I still had an hour to kill before boarding, so I decided the best thing to do would be to get a drink at the bar. In fact, I decided—and in retrospect this was not the most rational choice—that I should take a sleeping pill and have a few drinks. The bottle of pills warned that consumption of alcohol would increase the effect of the pill. In my fearful state, that sounded like the perfect solution: knocking myself out for the upcoming flight.

Forty minutes later, with three hefty South African beers under my belt and one pill down the old hatch, I was ready to jump on any plane of any kind. "Hydraulic problems? Landing gear not working? Who cares!" I said under my breath as we prepared to board. As we stepped out of the airport terminal and walked in the open air toward the stairs leading up into the huge jetliner, I gazed in my foggy haze at the gigantic tires on the plane. They seemed to be as big as me! I yelled at the man standing next to the plane, "Check those tires!" He looked concerned. I just laughed and staggered up the stairway, into the plane, and eventually into my seat. Once again I was in the upper compartment of the 747.

I don't remember much of what happened immediately after that. I know that the seat next to me was vacant, and that a girl in her early twenties sat one seat away by the window. I remember the takeoff. And I remember telling the girl what happened when we took off from JFK. She melted into tears when I told her about the emergency landing.

That surprised me, and I felt horrible. "Are you afraid of flying?"

She simply nodded like a little child.

I tried to comfort her. "These are the safest machines in the world. You are safer here than at home." It was no use. I realized I just had to shut up and leave her alone. I also found it ironic that I was trying to calm her down with data when it did me no good whatsoever. I was probably more afraid than she was, but was too drugged up to feel it.

The last thing I remember before falling asleep was looking into my bottle of sleeping pills and seeing that I only had one left. *This pill has to keep me knocked out on the second half of the trip,* I thought to myself. *I'll take it when we land to refuel on that little island.* I put the pill away and fell asleep.

I don't know how much time passed. It seemed like hours. I was not at all groggy from the pill or the alcohol when I woke up. I thought I had heard a loud thump, but when I opened my eyes, things seemed to be fine. The plane was fairly dark. The lights were turned low and the television monitor hanging from the ceiling above the closed cockpit door showed a map of the world and a little arrow pointing out our location over the sea. I strained my eyes and squinted to see where we were on the map. It looked like we were halfway across the ocean.

So far so good, I said to myself. *We're halfway home.* I leaned over and grabbed my briefcase from under the seat in front of me. I opened it and pulled out the little bottle of sleeping pills. I didn't know whether I should take the last one now or wait until we landed on that little island to refuel. When I opened the cap and looked inside, I was shocked to see that the bottle was empty. I gasped. Had I dropped the pill in my foggy haze? Had I taken the pill in my sleep? I gave a nervous laugh, realizing that I very well could have killed myself. *Wouldn't that be funny?* I thought. *Man dies of overdose trying to alleviate his fear of dying in a plane crash.* Regardless, the pill was gone, and I was a little miffed that I wouldn't be able to take another one to knock myself out again.

Just after putting my briefcase back under the seat in front of me and closing my eyes, it happened. BLAM! Weeeeeeeeeeee! Suddenly the plane was making the strangest sound.

This can't be! I said to myself, sitting up in my seat. *You've got to be freaking kidding!* I looked across the aisle at the other passengers. Some seemed oblivious to what was happening. Some looked up with concern. Then, suddenly, the plane took a sharp turn downward. It seemed to pick up speed, and the engine became very loud. The high-pitched whining sound continued, and I thought I heard the gurgling again. *Maybe he's trying to avoid turbulence,* I consoled myself. *Don't overreact, Grant. It's probably nothing. It's probably your imagination!* I looked across the aisle again. People were now paying attention. They looked scared. The plane picked up more speed, and I could hear a sound like a groan or a wail coming from the plane itself as the speed increased. The plane started shaking violently. I gasped, and others began to gasp and some to cry out.

The pilot's voice spouted out over the intercom. "We have an emergency. We are going to try to make it to an airport. Please put away any objects you may have in your possession and fasten your seat belts!"

"I can't believe it!" I whined as I curled up into a ball in my seat. The plane started to shake even more violently.

"Are you frightened?" the man next to me asked. I kept my face fixed downward, and similar to the girl earlier, I just nodded like a fearful child. His voice was comforting. He seemed so calm despite our circumstances. As for me, I began to shake in my seat. It was uncontrollable. I felt dizzy and thought I would pass out. The plane seemed to pick up even more speed, and the noise of the engines swelled.

Noticing my shaking, the man next to me nudged me and said, "If you want, you can hold my arm." I didn't hesitate for a moment. I needed to hold someone. I grabbed his arm and buried my face in his shoulder, shivering. He reminded me of my father. I held tight to his warm, strong arm.

Then the pilot came back on, shouting the words I feared: "Brace! Brace! Brace!"

"We're going to crash!" I cried.

"It's going to be OK." The man whose arm I held spoke calmly. He gently brushed my head with his other hand.

"What?" I said aloud. "We're crashing!" I pulled away from his arm and removed my face from his shirt. It was a red shirt. One I had seen before. I moved back to get a good look at the man who had comforted me. I shrieked in fear and disbelief. He had no face!

Cathunk. Weeeeeeeeeeeeeeee. Our plane touched down on the runway. "Welcome to Il de Sol. We have landed here only for refueling purposes. No one will be exiting the plane," the pilot announced in a calm, professional tone of voice. I shook my head and looked at the seat beside me. It was empty. The girl I had spoken with earlier was still one seat away, waking from her nap and stretching. The other passengers were calm and sedate. I looked at the empty seat beside me again. I couldn't believe it. It had been a dream.

When the plane came to a stop for refueling I couldn't sit still. Still shaking, I unbuckled and walked to the back of the upper compartment, down the steps to the lower level, and strolled down the aisle toward the back of the plane. I just needed to walk. As I looked over the mass of humanity that was on this plane, I broke into a cold sweat. I felt as if the people, the seats, the luggage, and the walls of the plane were closing in on me. We still had more than half the ocean to cross, and I didn't think I could stand being stuck there on that plane.

Thoughts tumbled through my mind. *What was that dream about? How horrible! To dream we were crashing while on a plane traversing the ocean—how cruel could the dream gods be? That man! That scary man! The ghost in the New Room? Free to follow me now? Meeting me on the plane? Damn! He isn't chained to the New Room anymore. This ghost has learned to haunt moving airplanes! I have to hand it to him. He fooled me. I thought he was my father for a moment.*

I was still shaking. How was I going to survive the rest of the flight? I didn't think I could fly anymore. Then I remembered the sleeping pill. I had dreamed it was gone, but it must still be there!

I hurried back to my seat and opened my briefcase. I pulled the bottle out and opened it. Yes! There it was, my comfort and my deliverer! I paused for a moment. I realized that I was falling fast into some sort of psychosis. The fear was too much. The dream was too real. The cold sweat was too wet. The trip was too long to endure without totally and utterly breaking down and running and jumping out the rear exit. I ordered a glass of wine. I gulped it down, took my pill, and fell back in my chair to sleep. Anything that I needed to work out or process, anything I needed to face, would have to wait until I landed in the United States and I was safely back at home. I wasn't going to think about anything else until then. That is, if I didn't die of some sort of overdose first. As I felt myself drifting off I was seized with overwhelming guilt. "Here we go again," I muttered to myself. Once again I was running from my fears, swallowing whatever I needed to swallow to avoid them. Once again I was fleeing the darkness and the void in my life—the terror and the lion's roar. It was too much for me. But I was so emotionally wrecked that I was ready to die rather than face the fear that was roaring in my ears on that jetliner crossing the ocean. I was awake when the plane took off, but soon after that I fell gently back to sleep.

The next thing I remember was being awakened by the flight attendant and handed a customs form to fill out before landing. The morning light streamed into the windows as people awoke, were served coffee, and readied themselves for landing. We were only a half hour from New York City. I had slept ten hours! When the plane touched down at JFK airport, I let out a long sigh of relief. I had made it!

As I walked off the plane I realized that I was weak, both physically and emotionally. Something had popped on that plane, and it wasn't the tire. It was something inside of me. Whatever had snapped was gurgling away inside. I had lost it. I didn't know if I'd ever get on another plane again. I didn't know if I'd ever travel anywhere again. As I walked to baggage claim, I wondered whether I'd ever leave home. I was shaking, tired, cold, and scared. I felt like I had been kicked in the chest and had no skin left to protect me. Yes, I was home, but I was gone emotionally.

PART 3

LACHY BROWN

10

HOME?

Not long after collecting my luggage and passing through customs, I stumbled out the door of the airport and into the sunny, breezy morning air. I stopped and breathed in America! America! It meant so much more to me now. I thanked God I was home and promised I would never take it for granted. Home!

I was met by three friends who had driven all the way from Philadelphia to New York City to pick me up. Nick, Stan, Jess, and I were all members of an unofficial men's support group that met biweekly to share our lives. We did a regular sweat-lodge ceremony every month or so, and had also gone away on a couple of weekends together. Knowing me well, they knew that the circumstances surrounding this trip were rough for me. They also knew that I'd have quite a story to tell. Driving all the way up there to bring me home was their way of showing support. Just seeing them gave me a new sense of comfort.

"Well, Mr. African Adventurer, what do you have to say for yourself?" asked Jess, the leader of the group and one of my closer friends. Like the rest of the men in my group, he was seemingly fearless and yet had an incredibly sensitive and empathetic heart. The men in the support group didn't fit into simple categories like "macho men" or, on the other extreme, "New Age sensitive guys." They had the best of both qualities. They were real warrior types with big hearts, or what I might call "New Age men with an edge."

"All I can say is, God bless America!" I responded. They laughed. After we piled my luggage in the car and began the long drive back to Philadelphia, I told them the entire story of my dramatic journey, beginning with the emergency landing at JFK and ending with my dream on the plane. They listened with empathy and excitement, as if they were living my adventure with me as I spoke. As I talked and they asked questions, I looked at the familiar scenery of my home country with new eyes. It felt odd to me that there were no bars and razor wire on homes we passed, that I didn't to have to stay in that constant state of awareness anymore. Inside, though, something seemed empty. I was safe again, and the overwhelming fear that gripped me to the marrow in South Africa was now gone, but now I felt as if my marrow was gone, too. It was a gnawing sensation, like a cancer eating away at the burned-out chasms of my being, a subtle terror that quietly ate away at my insides. This feeling would become more acute in the following days and stay with me for a long time.

As soon as the car pulled into our driveway, Cathy and the three older boys came bounding out of the house to greet me. Steven was still at school. We all hugged and smiled and hugged again. Ronnie, Jason, and Owen each had a story they wanted to share with me immediately. I felt so relieved to see them and Cathy that I hugged and kissed them and gave each one that look that said it all: *Wow! What was all that about? Aren't you glad it's over!*

As we spoke I noticed that the three men who had dropped me off were still there. They were leaning against the car enjoying the whole thing. They kept smiling and looking down the road and then back at me again. As I followed their gazes, I saw why they were waiting around. The crossing guard who stood at the end of our road and the policeman who first responded to Steven's accident were escorting little Steven across the road toward our home. They smiled as they directed Steven toward us, the same way my three escorts smiled. They knew full well this was our first greeting, and they were feeling what any parent would be feeling, knowing that a father and son were being reunited after escaping the clutches of death.

Steven dropped his school bag and ran to me. I bent down, caught him, and crushed him into my arms. "Steven. Steven. It's so good to see you! I am so glad to see you again! How are you feeling, Son?" The top of his head was wet from my tears.

He squeezed me back with his little arms and gently replied, "I'm fine, Dad. I don't even remember what happened.... I'm glad to see you too."

It felt good to hold Steven's warm body between my arms and to soak in his boyish spirit. I was so thankful to be able to see him and hold him again. I didn't want to let go. As we continued to hug I glanced over Steven's shoulder and saw the policeman give a nod, then hop in his car and drive away. The three men who had escorted me from the airport smiled proudly, satisfied with what they witnessed, then climbed into their car and drove away. Cathy and the other boys came over and surrounded us in a group hug. Even our dog barked inside the door as if to say, "Hey, don't forget about me!" I held all my boys for quite some time in silence. We were all so happy to be safely reunited again.

Soon we walked inside to sit down and talk about all that had happened. Each boy was given as much time as needed to express what he had experienced with Steven's accident and how he was feeling now. Cathy and I also shared our feelings. I would never wish for anyone else to experience the circumstances that brought us to this level of sharing, but I will say that it was an incredible time of love and bonding.

The days that followed with Cathy and the boys were both deeply meaningful and fulfilling. It seemed that coming so close to death and loss made it easier for me to appreciate even the most seemingly insignificant things about them. Ronnie's curly hair looked so much cuter. Jason's laugh brought delight. Owen's smile could bring me to tears. And any idiosyncrasy from Steven would emotionally drop me in my tracks. I had a nagging feeling that we may have cheated death, but perhaps not for long. Death was looking for us, and who knows when he would find us? My mother's lessons from childhood had come back in full force: "This is not a safe world. Anything can happen. Snap! Just like that!" So I counted my blessings and sucked in the joys of life every moment I could before death showed up to even the score. I did this in weakness, and I did this in trepidation.

When I had a chance to stop by and visit my mother and father, my eldest sister, Beth Ann, met me coming out the door. She had always been very quiet and composed and kept mostly to herself. But after welcoming me home, she pulled me aside and told me that this whole experience with Steven had really jolted our parents. She said that it had brought back some things that they hadn't dealt with for years. I noticed that she was trembling as she spoke to me. "I was shaken by it," she continued. "It reminded me of when I was a child. I was the only one, you know. Nobody would talk about it then. It's all coming back now." I gathered she was speaking about Bruce. She was the only other sibling at the time of his death, and I wondered what it must have been like for her. She had never mentioned it—ever! The three members of our family who had been alive when my brother passed, Mom, Dad, and Beth Ann, simply never spoke about what had happened.

"Oh, Beth Ann. What do you mean? Are you OK?"

"I don't know. I can hardly talk about it. We've never been able to talk about it, Grant. And now it's all suddenly come to the surface. Just be gentle with her. She can't take it. Just let that part about Bruce be. OK?"

"Sure. I understand."

"Maybe you do," Beth Ann replied. "There is so much we could talk about sometime. But not now. I don't think any of us can take any more. Not yet. It seems like we just need a break, let everything settle down again. Things have been so weird lately.... I've got to go." She abruptly ended the conversation, looked back at my parents' house, and then disappeared down the path. This was so unlike her. I found it very disturbing. I wanted to pursue her to find out what on earth was going on, but obviously she was in a lot of emotional pain, so I decided to let her go.

Both my mother and father were delighted to see me and greeted me warmly. I thanked them again for taking care of Steven. I sat and shared with them about my adventures in South Africa, about the knobkerrie and Kosan's stories. I talked to them about the flight as well, and also about the fears and the dreams. These were, after all, my parents. It was impossible not to show them the wounded and scared child I hid inside. I shared everything I had been experiencing. Dad became silent, not really knowing how to respond to another man's weakness. Mom tried to comfort me, telling me to be strong, to give myself some time. But I could sense her own fear. I knew that while trying to comfort me she was also trying to comfort herself. I saw very quickly what Beth Ann had been speaking about. It made me deeply sad and concerned.

"I haven't been able to shake the fear, Mom," I said. "I feel like I've been shocked or something. I'm raw. I thought it would go away, but I keep feeling like something bad is going to happen. It's like the darkness won't go away. I think I'm losing it. Really," I confessed.

"I know. I know!" she replied. "They say you don't have to worry, but you do. If you stop worrying, that's when things happen." She swallowed hard with these words and then put on a determined expression. "You've got to be strong! You just have to keep on going! That's what I was always taught, and it works, you know." I saw that she was trying as hard as possible not to lose control. She took a deep breath. "Anyone can be taken any time. Just like that. . . . You just have to live with that."

Hearing those words made me feel sad and sorry for her. It also gave me the chills, because this had been the message about life since my youth. I had never felt so much in tune with her woeful words. I sensed the darkness closing in, and in those shadows I felt the growing presence of doom.

"I don't think I can fly anymore. Mom, Dad, if I have to quit my job will you be there for me? I don't think I can do it anymore."

"Don't be ridiculous," Dad barked with his usual gruffness, but also a sense of underlying love. "They won't fire you just because you can't fly. Maybe you could do something else. Give yourself some time! Time is a healer, Son."

"No, it isn't!" snapped my mother in a low voice.

"Oh, Bette, don't start again," Dad replied.

"No. I won't. I will never start again!" Mom murmured as she quickly left the room and headed toward her bedroom.

"She's a little shaken up, Son. No more talk about death, OK? She can't take it. We've always been there if you needed us. Don't worry about it. Now you'd better go."

I left the house and headed back home. Mom was in so

much pain. Unable to deal with it, I could only focus on my own. And yet somehow I felt, I knew, I was carrying it all.

When I arrived home I sat down at the picnic table outside our kitchen door. At that moment, a commercial plane flew overhead, and the sound of the jet engines made me sick. I thought I might throw up right there. I remembered everything that had transpired, all the fear, the pain. I never wanted to fly again. I never wanted to leave home again. I never wanted to lose sight of my children again. But what was the use of even thinking these things when it could all end in a moment? Snap! Just like that. I buried my head in my arms, strung out with despair and emotionally exhausted.

11

LAUREL CAMP

Several weeks after my return from South Africa, my fears hadn't diminished. If anything, they had increased. Not a day went by that I did not think about how quickly life can end, and the thought made me feel sick inside. I knew that my job didn't call for me to fly for a couple more months, but this didn't seem to give me much comfort. When I heard the jet engines of a distant plane flying overhead, a feeling of dread would come over me. I kept remembering that horrible dream, the captain's command to brace, and the faceless man. It all seemed too real and too foreboding.

I found myself needing to stay close to home more and more, to be with my children, especially Steven. He seemed to want to stay close to me as well, giving me extra hugs, waltzing into our bedroom and flopping on the bed beside me to share a television show. Each time I hugged him or looked into his innocent eyes, I was engulfed by an overwhelming sense of impending doom. The heavy reality of death hung in the air. It was hanging around the whole family, and it wouldn't go away.

Those two close brushes with death, the dreams, the time of heightened awareness in Soweto, it all forced me to redefine life as one very precious moment in this universe of ours. It was a moment to be cherished and remembered. Each day I found myself gazing upon my children a little longer. Every time they ran out the door to go and play I took a snapshot of them in my mind, in case it was my last. I didn't do it deliberately. The shutter inside my head just kept snapping these pictures on its own, intermittently during the day—the boys smiling, laughing, running down the street, eating supper, silently sleeping in their little beds. The mental photo album grew and grew. Soon I was uncontrollably snapping mental photos of everyone, assessing their personal meaning to me in this world, and forming a mental caption to remember them by. Those old words kept haunting me: at any moment this whole world could come crashing down and it would be all over.

Though time passed, I was not getting a grip on my fear. To deal with the anxiety, I started up my old habit of smoking a pipe again. I found myself in most of my free time sitting at the picnic table outside our kitchen door puffing on my pipe and watching the planes fly overhead. With everything that had happened, I seriously thought I might see one fall out of the sky if I watched long enough. I felt like my life had suddenly fallen out of the sky. I had, in effect, already crashed and burned. The fire was now out, but I was charred. I literally felt like my skin had been burned off, exposing my raw insides. No protection. I could feel too much. I could sense too much. I felt as if I was loving too much, so much that I grieved at the possibility of losing my loved ones, as if it were imminent.

The one hopeful thing on the immediate horizon was that another Laurel Camp was coming up very soon. Our family would be attending, and I would be the pastor there. This was that annual church family camp where a lot of good healing took place for me, and also for many who go there. It was located in the beautiful mountains of western Pennsylvania, a real paradise and a place of peace. The theme of the camp this year was belonging. That theme seemed appropriate because I needed to connect with someone, anyone who would give me some comfort, and perhaps some courage to face my fears. Laurel Camp was a place for spiritual connection and recuperation. The people there would understand my fears, and they were people I could confide in without fear of being judged or viewed as emotionally weak.

This year we were preparing for a three-week trip away from home. We would head out to Laurel Hill State Park, where the camp was held, for a week, and then from there we would head off for a two-week vacation in Hazelhurst, Wisconsin, our vacation spot in the Northwoods. I had high hopes that these next three weeks would be the perfect break for the whole family and would bring me some much-needed healing.

As we pulled into the green, wooded camp at Laurel Hill my nostrils and my whole being were filled with its scents. It was thick with a mossy wetness, a bit of smoke from a nearby fire, and the faint smell of cooking food drifting from the nearby camp kitchen. The wind gently moved through the trees as the distant voices of children playing in the woods echoed here and there. In many ways I felt like I was home, especially this year. Many of my good friends were here. Hopefully I could relax in this beautiful mountain setting and, surrounded by such a caring community, perhaps even get to a deeper level than I had so far.

I was especially looking forward to seeing Dottie Ellenger. She was a vivacious mother of four in her late forties. I could describe her as a psychiatrist, social worker, massage therapist, herbal expert, and dabbler in any and all New Age practices, but the best way to describe Dottie is "Shaman Mom." She was a crazy sort of second mother to me. We had worked together at church camps before, and she always reserved a time to do some loving experiment on me, whether that was energy work, counseling, herbal remedies, or whatever she felt was appropriate for the visit. She was always jovial, had a good laugh, and showed immense compassion and warmth. Dottie was also, contrary to her practices, a very down-to-earth woman. She often offered me the type of practical, motherly wisdom that I needed to keep me grounded and set me on a good course. Two years earlier she used a combination of hypnotism and Reiki, a modern form of energy healing, to help me stop smoking. I left her "operating table" never to touch tobacco again, until, as I have said, a week after returning from South Africa. Dottie had set aside a full afternoon midweek to work her magic on me. I was excited to see what this would bring—maybe a little hypnotherapy combined with whatever else she had up her sleeve. I had an idea that if she could get me to stop smoking she could help me get over my fears.

Besides Dottie, there were many special people gathered at this church camp. It would take a full week just to sit down and really have a good talk with each of them. One particular man who happened to be at camp this week was Lachy Brown. He was a quiet and gentle man in his late forties, married to a longtime friend of mine, Dorothy. Together they had eight children: three born to them and five adopted. It was obvious that they loved children, and they had what seemed to be unlimited energy to care for them. In fact, their care for people in general was something to behold and to honor. I found out that Lachy would be in my particular sharing group this year, and I looked forward to getting to know him better. He lived not too far from me—in fact, he grew up less than a block away from our house—but our paths never seemed to cross over the years except at Laurel Camp.

A year ago, he had come up to me after my camp lecture and commented on my talk. He said, "Gee, Grant, this year you see a message from God on a sign by the roadside? What will happen next year? Will you see the Goodyear Blimp overhead flashing the message, 'Grant, do this'?" I still remembered his words and his gentle smile. I myself had wondered what the message would be this year. I sure needed a blimp—as long as I didn't have to fly in it.

When I met up with him at this year's camp he looked relaxed. A stocky man with a three-day beard, he had something of the look of a mountain man about him. We shook hands and I reminded him of his words a year before, promising him I had some good stories this year, and maybe a blimp would be in one. He looked puzzled, not remembering our conversation the year before.

"You must be thinking of someone else," he replied, concerned. "I don't remember saying that. But that doesn't mean I didn't say it. I don't always remember things like I used to. Getting older, I suppose. But I do know life can get pretty strange sometimes. Hey, we're in the same group this year! That's great! I'm looking forward to us spending some good time together."

Each member of camp was officially assigned to a sharing group made up of eight to ten people who would meet for two hours daily. It was sort of like a daily twelve-step group, a place to check in and to talk about life. It was the bread and butter of the camp, a time when people really got to know each other and bonded as they shared the trials and tribulations of human existence.

I was looking forward to spending some time with Lachy, too. In fact, as we talked, I felt something moving in my heart, almost a yearning. I needed support in a bad way. I needed courage. I needed an older man to talk to. I sensed that he'd make a good big brother to lay some heavy stuff on. I really wanted to be around him and pick up some of the peace of mind and calm that seemed to emanate from his character.

After two days at camp, I had shared with many people that I was truly in some serious emotional trouble. The sum total of wisdom I had received so far was that one friend grabbed me after a brief conversation about my mental condition and said, "You know, Grant, many spiritual leaders and scholars point to your state as an ideal. We're supposed to be in touch with death. That way we can learn how to live." I thanked him verbally, but inside I was a bit peeved. Did he not understand the anguish I was in? I wasn't in any spiritual state. I was sick. I wouldn't wish this on anyone.

By the time I had the floor to share about my life in my group, most of the members had already heard of our frightening flight back to JFK and about Steven's miraculous escape from death. As I took them through the story I could see that they were on that plane with me, and they grieved with me as I shared the feelings I experienced finding out from thousands of miles away that my little boy had been hit by a bus. I told them about my mother's fears and how they had affected me, and how I had passed those fears on to my own children. "I thought I dealt with this years ago, but now it's back."

"What made your mother so afraid?" a voice asked from across the dimly lit room. It was Lachy.

"She had a son who died before I was born. He caught pneumonia and died rather suddenly. I guess when I came along, I looked a lot like him, and she didn't want the same thing to happen again," I replied in a matter-of-fact tone.

"What was his name?" Lachy asked.

"Bruce."

"And he died before you were born. So you never knew him?"

"That's right. I've seen his picture, but my parents never really talked too much about him. All Dad ever said was that they buried him in his little cowboy boots." My voice trembled with those words. It must have been so tough for Dad and Mom. I could still see Dad's face twist and hold back the grief when he shared with me that one piece of information about his son's death.

"So all this fear your mother felt, she unconsciously put that into you again and again as you were growing up?" His voice was very gentle, almost pastoral in tone.

"Yeah, I guess. But I thought I had dealt with that. I guess I was wrong. I think the airplane experience rubbed me raw, and then when Bruce got hit by the bus it all came back to me," I replied, deep in the memories.

"How did Bruce die?" Lachy asked with a sense of purpose in his voice.

"He caught pneumonia. Didn't I just say that?" I replied, a little perplexed.

"What you just said was that Bruce was hit by a bus."

"No. Steven was hit by the bus."

"Yes, but you said Bruce."

He was right, and it suddenly occurred to me that I had done this a week before in talking to Cathy. At that time she said, "You mean Steven," with a bit of anger in her voice. And I had simply corrected myself and moved on with the conversation. But to make this mistake twice in less than two weeks? What was going on here?

"Oh, wow. This is the second time I've done that. What does this mean? Am I somehow mixing Bruce up with Steven?" Something deep inside my stomach resonated with those words. There was a truth in that statement that I couldn't completely grasp yet. I knew in my gut that I was on to something important. "I know that Bruce's death is related to some of my fears.

Maybe this really is just about that old childhood fear of dying. It's got to be a core issue, don't you think?" There was a moment of silence while I contemplated these things. "I had finally convinced myself that this is a safe world, but it's not. It's not! It's not safe. Anything can happen any time. Cathy and I just looked at each other on that plane and asked, 'Why, God?' For days I've asked him that question. Why? What were you trying to prove? That you can take anybody out just like that? How would that help me? I'm afraid someone is going to die. I know it's all in my head, but . . ."

"Hey, if it's a core issue," one of the women said, "then wouldn't it make sense that it's been reawakened? Give yourself some time."

"Yeah, I know. I just need a break, but I feel like something inside just isn't right. You know, sometimes you can identify some problem and maybe you have trouble working with it, but at least you can see it. I feel like I'm just not seeing it all. It's deep. Really deep."

Lachy waited for a moment to see if I was finished and then added, "It's going to clear up, Grant. Give it time. Hey, if those things happened to me, I'd be feeling the same way you're feeling. You know, I fly for a living. There are those times when it gets a little hairy in that chopper and I think of a lot of possibilities, and they're not all comforting."

I had forgotten that Lachy was a pilot. I wondered whether part of my yearning to know him better was to learn more about flying. Maybe I wanted some of that pilot experience to rub off on me. I made a mental note that I really did need to set aside a time with him to talk. I could ask him about flying, and perhaps the more I learned the less frightened I'd be.

There were a few more words from the others, but then we had to close the meeting and prepare for the evening worship service coming up shortly. That was fine with me. Talking about it brought relief. I got what I needed for the time being—at least a bit of an insight into this whole dilemma.

It seemed so obvious, and yet it eluded me. The reason I felt so bad was that I had been truly shaken. Because of the two jarring brushes with death, the childhood fears within me were reawakened. That explained the terrible dream about the ghost in the New Room and the nightmare on the plane back from South Africa. Since these were core issues about life and death, they weren't going to just go away. I had to give them time. There was more to these deep feelings of fear than I could understand at the moment. There was a missing piece to all of it. I had no clue what that piece was, but it was as if the darkness, the darkness of death that I feared so much, was following me around for a reason. It was as if there was purpose behind it, a message for my soul, a lesson to be learned. I just didn't know what that lesson was, and I feared the darkness and any deeper message it might have for me.

I was tired. The two weeks up in the Northwoods looked more and more inviting to me. That would be just the rest I needed. And before that time I could get some healing here. In fact, as I left the cabin to head back to main camp, I remembered Dottie. Tomorrow she would do her magic on me, and who knew what insights might pop out while under her care? In this raw, emotional state, it could be big.

12

A PUSH FROM BEYOND

The day had arrived for my rendezvous with Dottie. This year she had set up her makeshift office in a very small room adjacent to the main camp garage. It was more like a large closet with a door on one side and a window on the other. Her massage table sat square in the middle of the room. Two scented candles burned on a nearby shelf, and quiet, calming music flowed from a portable CD player next to them. As I entered that room, I sensed immediately that she had worked hard to make this place hospitable, even inviting. I felt a sense of peace and safety surrounding me.

I sat on her massage table.

"What can I do for you today?" Dottie asked with a devilish grin. She loved experimenting on me. Whether through quiet meditations, energy work, hypnosis, or just listening, she had a nurturing way about her that exuded motherhood—comfort, love, support, healing. When I visited Dottie for these sessions each year it seemed to make such a difference to my sense of well-being. She was almost like a mechanic, opening me up, fixing a few inner parts, welding the broken pieces, and then putting me back together again.

The first time she had done energy work on me, I immediately had the deep sense that I was a soldier back from a long battle and she was the medic whose job it was to put me back together. The fear of death that seemed to surround me began to temporarily dissipate as I anticipated what might happen today in her care.

"I need some major help today."

"Oh yeah?"

"Yes. I'm dying from fear. You heard about the incident over JFK and what happened to Steven. I feel like I'm in panic mode all the time. I seriously doubt I'll ever be able to fly again. I'm worried the fear is going to paralyze me completely. Got any ideas, Doc?"

"Well, a relaxing meditation couldn't hurt. What else did you have in mind? We could try hypnosis. I cured someone the other day of a phobia using hypnosis. It works well with some people."

"I was thinking the same thing. Remember when you cured me of smoking?"

"Yeah, I saw you smoking your pipe last night. Some good that did!"

"No, it did work. You helped me quit. I had no withdrawal symptoms at all after our session. I started all on my own about a month ago or less. Seriously. That stuff works on me."

"I'm willing if you're willing," Dottie replied cheerfully.

Dottie and I talked for about a half hour before she started to work her magic on me. We talked about the airplane incident, and about Steven's close call, and we both said a little prayer to find peace and meaning in these terrible memories. We wondered together why these incidents had happened one after another, like a double punch to the stomach. Was there some deeper reason? As we shifted into a quiet meditation, she put on some soft music and began to relax me for hypnosis.

"You are now stepping backward, into the deep. Take three steps. One. Good. It's getting darker, more peaceful. Two. All is quiet." Her voice was comforting and growing faint. "Three. There. You are in a deep state of peace."

As I listened to her comforting words and the music, I drifted in and out of unrelated thoughts. After a while I gave myself permission to go to sleep. I don't know how much I missed, but as I lay on the table I got the distinct impression I had awakened from a dream. I clearly felt that I had awakened to another world, even though everything looked the same. The feelings in me and around me changed. I knew that, in fact, my heart was being opened. I began to feel a deep sense of meaning, and my imagination ran wild with vivid images. In my mind's eye I had returned to South Africa, surrounded by masses of people. I saw both the poverty and the opulence, the brotherhood and the strife, the peace of mind and the political turmoil, the joy and the pain of their existence. In this land of extremes the best and the worst of life, humanity, and reality itself existed side by side. But in my trancelike vision I could see that these two contrasts did not coexist peacefully. There was, indeed, a great gulf between them. The light of integrity struggled against the darkness of human want. Compassion fought to gain the upper hand over indifference. I not only understood but felt the veracity of Mablevi Buthelezi's words: "The real battle is the one taking place right now all over the world, between what is right and wrong, good and evil." I could sense that this was true not only in South Africa, where the contrasts seemed more overt than in other places, but all over the world! Underneath the images, behind the appearances of this world, a battle was raging—an unseen warfare. Along with the images, thoughts started coming. As they flashed quickly through my mind I relayed them to her.

"Dottie, I understand now."

"Oh, yeah? Tell me." Her gentle, feminine voice was comforting.

"Dottie." Tears began to seep out of the sides of my eyes and run down my temples toward my ears, "There's not enough love in the world. There are so many lonely, desperate people in pain. I just want to help people so that they can feel love. I need more love. We all need more love." I let myself be silent and stay with the state, gathering the feelings and thoughts as they came to me. Dottie sat quietly beside me, listening.

I continued, "There's a struggle taking place for every human soul."

"Yes, but isn't everyone involved in their own personal struggle?" Dottie asked as she placed her hands over my heart to begin some energy work.

"Perhaps, but only some are aware. Others are asleep. So many are sleeping right through their lives. They're not using what they've been given."

"What have they been given? Talents?"

"It's more like power! I keep getting the strong message, 'Don't be afraid of your power.' I think I'm supposed to tell you that too. You've got power. Don't be afraid of it."

"I know. Because it's not mine to begin with," Dottie replied in a contemplative voice.

"No. It belongs to the Divine. But don't hide it or be afraid to use it fully."

"Grant, weird things have been happening to me. This is powerful stuff I'm working with now. I have become more afraid of it as it's grown. I keep thinking maybe I should back off. You know that the connection between the spiritual and natural worlds is closer than we think. It's right here. Sometimes that's scary, and I wonder what I'm doing. But I know at the same time how useful my work has been to people."

"Yes, and it's important that you continue your work. And Dottie—" I was interrupted by the CD player, which began skipping through the meditative song that was playing.

"Oh drat! Hang on." Dottie fumbled with it, and it began to work again.

"I feel like I'm being called. I mean like someone is literally calling me or wants to meet me. I'm not sure what it means.... I think I'm supposed to be working with someone. I don't know if I need to help them, or they'll help me, or both. I don't know what they'll do, what they're supposed to do, or what I'm supposed to do when I find them, but it's urgent. Um, I think you can help me with this. I get the strangest impression that you can help me identify this person. But who is it?" In this altered state I searched the darkness for names or faces. I saw the faces of the men and women in Africa, my wife, my sons, and others. I saw faces of people I didn't know, of all races and nationalities.

After a time one face emerged from the rest. It was the face of Lachy Brown. I could clearly see his rough, pleasant face smiling in the darkness. It seemed he was one I certainly needed to talk to. But was this a message from above or simply my own mind playing tricks with me? I had already recognized my attraction to his calming presence, and had already made a mental note to set up a time to talk with him about flying. Perhaps the name Lachy Brown was too obviously of my own unconscious needs and desires. I began to doubt whether this session was doing anything for me or whether it was just a gratuitous trip to my own unconscious mind.

Dottie interrupted these thoughts as she held her hand a few inches from my heart and it began to flutter. It fluttered so much that it tickled, and I told her with a giggle to knock it off.

She smiled and continued her work. "Where are you getting these ideas from?" she asked. "Are you seeing things? Hearing things?"

I thought about it. I wasn't sure. In one sense, I was seeing images, but in another sense, it seemed someone was feeding me these ideas and images. "It's as if someone is just giving them to me, like some whispering angels. I sense a lot of love in these whispers."

"Can you see someone? Is it a person, or just a voice? Is it male or female?"

Before I could even reflect on her questions, the CD player went haywire, flipping through songs, starting one, changing to another. Dottie turned away. "What is wrong with this thing?" She reached over and shut it off.

Something about that CD player going haywire gave me a chill. Ghost from the New Room? Whatever it was, the noise brought me back to full awareness. I just popped out of the trancelike state as if waking from a dream. I knew I wasn't going to be able to get back to it, either. "It's over. Just let me sit with it for a while." I fell silent and lay limp on the table. Another ten minutes passed in silence until the dinner bell rang, calling all in the camp to supper. We had to debrief from our experience quickly. The group was expecting me to make announcements during dinner.

As I sat up on the table, I said, "Dottie, there's some sort of struggle going on. I suppose this is nothing new, but more love is needed in the world. We don't have to struggle alone with this. I got the sense that there's a lot of help being offered if only we ask, or believe, or something. We can do so much more if we are not afraid."

We both paused for a moment and then chuckled, suddenly aware that what we were saying must surely seem like nonsense to anyone else in the world.

"Oh, well. So much for Star Wars," I said, throwing off the whole afternoon as if it were nothing more than watching a good movie. "I guess we'll find out more next time. But I'm going to keep my eyes open, and I'd appreciate it if you did too. After all, I got the impression that you're going to point somebody out to me, somebody I need to see, maybe work with?"

"Ha ha! Well, Luke Skywalker, let me think for a moment." She stopped me from getting off the table. "How about Lachy Brown?" In one way her answer was shocking, because Lachy was just the person who had come to me. But Lachy was also a reasonable guess. He was one of the more open-minded campers, and there seemed to be some sort of glow about him this year.

"Funny you should say that. I thought of him as well. He certainly looks like he has a story to tell. But I already wanted to talk to him. Something tells me he's a great guy but not necessarily on some spiritual quest, or the one I'm looking for. I'll feel him out when I get a chance to talk to him."

"How about Bob Vercelli?"

"Nah."

"Tim Schmucker."

"Nope."

"How about Stan Morey? He's a spiritual guy."

"Hey, just because someone is a spiritual guy doesn't mean they're called to save the world! Cut me a break. You just named four guys. Think about it for a while."

"OK. OK. I'll think about it. . . . Maybe it's a woman? Cathy is too obvious. How about . . ."

"Dottie!"

"Got it. I'll get back to you on this," she responded with a smile.

I smiled too and gave her a hug. "And thanks, Dottie. It was a wonderful experience."

Thus ended my rendezvous with Dottie.

13

SILVER STAR

The next morning I awoke to the sound of two squirrels quarreling in a tree near our cabin. Cathy had already left for an early morning prayer meeting, and the four boys slept quietly in their bunks. I woke them to prepare for breakfast and the day ahead. This was the last full day of Laurel Camp. Tonight we would have a special ceremony with the teens in camp. There were about forty of them, approximately twenty girls and twenty boys. It was a larger crowd than usual, and we wanted to do something special with them. We had come up with a plan to take the boys off with the men of the camp to a distant fire, where we would talk and have a time to honor those men who had made a difference in our lives. The women would do something similar at their own fire. I was especially excited about this because my older two sons, Ronnie and Jason, would be there. I wouldn't just be Dad out there. I'd be their brother. That was important to me, because I knew they needed support from me, not just as a father, but as a man, friend, and brother. As they grew older, I looked forward to being their friend and brother, not just for their sake, but for my own. I never had a brother to walk beside me, to share the experience of life's path. As they grew each day, I saw the potential for that relationship to develop and that time to come. Tonight would be a good start.

We left the cabin together and enjoyed breakfast with the rest of the campers. While others ate an assortment of eggs, pancakes, fruit, and cereal, I usually had a cup of coffee and a fresh pipe full of tobacco. This was an old and not-so-healthy custom I had inherited from my father, who began the day with three cups of coffee and half a pack of cigarettes.

The mood of the camp was extremely pleasant. The theme of "belonging" wasn't just something we talked about this week. We tried to live it. I had the sense that most felt very much like they belonged and were cared for. At the end of the morning session, the camp director reminded people that since this was the last day, there might be some people we still wanted to talk to. This was our last opportunity. As he reminded me of that I reflected that I still hadn't gotten some time to chat with Lachy Brown. But he was not present in this gathering. I knew that this afternoon would be my only chance, so I searched for his wife, Dorothy, in the hope that she would know where I could find him to set up a time. I didn't have to look far. Dorothy was standing right in front of me, talking with one of her sons. I broke in.

"Hey Dorothy, where's Lachy?"

"He's with Dottie," she said as she hugged her son and sent him on his way.

"Oh, yeah?" I wondered what this was about.

"Yeah. He was really excited. He wanted a massage but so many people signed up before him that she was all booked up. Jenny had to cancel her session early this morning and Dottie let Lachy take her place. So he's with Dottie. It shouldn't be too long. He's been in there for a while." Dorothy pointed toward the garage in the main camp.

As I walked down to main camp I watched the camp garage for any signs of Lachy Brown appearing from Dottie's healing chamber. I just had to talk with him before it was too late. I had shared a great deal this entire week, and Dottie's healing session had brought me some peace along with some complex questions, but I still had that sense of gnawing fear inside. Something in me was churning, crying for help, reaching for some sort of answer. I wasn't sure what the question was. It was that old blackness, the emptiness I had felt so often before. In that darkness lay my deepest fears: death, the void, the unknown. Maybe time would heal me. I didn't know. But if time couldn't bring me a cure, I wasn't sure what else would.

As I walked in deep thought, breathing in the still-fresh morning air and waving to the children who had broken into a spontaneous game of stick ball between the public bathrooms and the dining hall, I heard a distant door slam over in the direction of the camp garage. I looked over and saw Dottie hurrying up the driveway toward me. She was pointing at me in a poking fashion, the way a teacher might be scolding a student. But she was grinning from ear to ear. And as she came closer I saw that the grin was mixed with a slight bit of urgency.

"What is it, Dottie?"

She stopped in front of me and paused to catch her breath. "It's Lach," she said.

"It's locked? What's locked?" From the curious concern on her face I thought she might have accidentally locked her keys in her car or maybe jammed the door shut to her massage room.

"No, stupid!" she said with a laugh. "Not Lock. Lock key! It's Lachy Brown!"

"What about him?" I asked, a little embarrassed about my mistake.

"Go see him!" she commanded. "He has got to be the one."

"What did he say?" I looked toward the garage, expecting him to emerge at any moment.

"Look, you're going to have to ask him. You told me to tell you if I found anyone, and Lachy is definitely into this stuff. You've got to talk to him."

"OK, I will." I turned to go past her toward the garage. "Thanks."

She gave a girlish giggle, turned, and headed off to the main cabin. I think her laughter signified her recognition that this was part of our little "otherworld" game. I sensed a message in her laughter not to take this all too seriously. Smiling, I pointed my finger toward the garage and then headed toward it to find Lachy. As I reached the door to Dottie's chamber, I paused. I stared at the door. I felt a sense of uneasiness rising up within me. Opening that door suddenly seemed frightening to me. I didn't know what was behind that door. Something about my childhood experience with ghosts and doors in the New Room gave me pause. Would Lachy be on the other side of that door, or would there be a faceless man there to greet me? I stood motionless.

I could always knock and let him open it, I thought to myself, *or I could just wait here until he comes out.* That seemed like a good plan. I waited for a moment, then changed my mind. *Maybe I should knock.* I reached up to knock when a voice startled me.

"Grant!" the voice cried, over in the direction of a picnic table in a clearing thirty yards away. It was Lachy's voice.

"Grant!" Lachy called again as he sat on the table with his hands folded in front of him. "Hey, come over here!" He hadn't been in the room after all. I was relieved that I didn't have to open that door. I jogged over to the table to greet him.

"Hey, I've wanted to talk to you all week," he said. "How about now?"

He looked a little worn out, as if he had been jogging all morning. "I see Dottie's done a number on you," I said, shaking his hand. I was glad to know that the desire to talk was mutual.

He grabbed my hand tightly. "She is amazing! I see why people line up to get a session with her," he responded. "I'm ready for a nap. But we should talk. You said you wanted to talk about flying, didn't you? Well, why not now? Nobody will bother us here. You got time?" He jumped up from the table and stood in front of me. I didn't remember actually telling him about my desire to learn about flying from him, but he could have picked that up from our group session the other night. Regardless, his offer to talk seemed like a gift.

"Yes, I've got time. All the time in the world! But what happened in there with Dottie?"

"That's kind of personal." He smiled and lit up a Camel cigarette, the kind without the filters. Lachy sort of fit that image of the smoking cowboy, the Marlboro Man, with perhaps a little aging and a slightly softer complexion. He sat down opposite me on the other side of the picnic table. I accepted his answer with my silence and pulled out my pipe, stuffed it with some fresh tobacco, and lit up.

"So you want to know about flying, do you?" he asked. "I've been flying choppers since 'Nam. What sort of things would you like to know?"

I asked him about turbulence and flying into bad weather. I asked him about backup systems and hydraulics. He talked openly and very informatively about the ups and downs of flying. He went on at length, but paused from time to time to see if he was keeping my interest or meeting my needs. Then he stopped and said, "Grant, it looks to me like you need to talk about something. What is it?"

As he had been explaining flying I had been feeling like

that wasn't really what I wanted from him, but I didn't know what it was that I did want. That longing came back, and perhaps the sense that even learning more about this man's life would somehow give me the courage to face my own. He exuded bravery, and I wanted some of that to rub off on me. Never mind Dottie's prompting to see him or what my otherworldly experience might mean. I wanted to hear all about Lachy's life and soak in every bit of it.

"You were in Vietnam? Can you tell me about that?" I was hoping to hear a story or two about the war that might give me some courage.

"Yes, I was in Vietnam, but I don't often talk about it. Why do you want to know?" He seemed reluctant to share his experience.

"Oh, I don't know. I guess I've always been interested in that war, and a soldier's life in general."

"Well, you're sort of in a war yourself, aren't you?" he remarked in a matter-of-fact manner as he crushed his cigarette and placed the butt in his front pocket for later disposal.

"Did Dottie tell you?" I asked.

"About what?"

"About our little 'otherworld' experience."

"No. I did all the talking in there. Life's been getting weird lately."

"You can bet on that," I said.

"No, what I meant before was that just like I was a soldier in Vietnam, you're a spiritual soldier now. I think there are probably a lot of similarities between what I went through and what you're going through. I mean, you fight battles every day as a spiritual leader, don't you?"

"I suppose."

"That's the real battle. You've been pretty beat up by it, too. Don't let those bastards bring you down. I mean, the whole plane ride and your son and all that, don't let the enemy break you down. There's a greater power on your side, you know."

I nodded. His words were direct hits on my heart, assaulting my fears. I didn't know whether he was just lucking out or whether somehow this Lachy Brown guy knew the whole story of my life and was sent to give me the answer. I opted for the more rational explanation for the time being, but I tested him.

"Yes. It's a war out there. You must be fighting that war too?"

"You're not kidding! Yes, it's been a rough year. I've fought with everything I have. I'm doing OK. I'm still alive. But that's enough about me. What about you? What's going on with you and Dottie?" he asked.

I decided the only way I was going to find out if he were the person I had felt called to find was to tell him the story. I started off by telling him that I don't usually believe in a lot of mumbo jumbo, but that some strange things took place in my session with Dottie. He stopped me at one point to assure me that hearing about strange things didn't scare him.

"Lachy," I continued, "I get the impression I'm supposed to meet someone, or get to know someone for some purpose. I don't know what that means, or who it is, or why. But it's real, and I get a deep impression that it's urgent."

"So, what do you think?" Lachy asked. "Think I'm part of this? Is it me? Is that why you're staring at me with that funny smile?"

In fact, I had that exact unspoken question. I just kept silent.

"Maybe I am the one. I don't know," he responded. "Maybe there is someone you need to get to know to fulfill some destiny, or many people. And it could be that there's something inside you that you need to get in touch with. I'm not going to discount what you are saying. I want to think about it. Lately

I've felt that the world can get awfully strange, even incredible."

"Like how?"

"Well, I suppose since you shared with me, I'll share with you. This is going to sound nuts."

"Probably no more nuts than what I shared."

"Yeah. But maybe we're both nuts. That's no consolation. Anyway, while Dottie was working on me, I came into such a spiritual state that I felt compelled to share with her something amazing that had happened to me. Maybe I'm supposed to share it with you. Have you ever been in a Native American sweat lodge?"

"Yeah, believe it or not, I've got one in my backyard."

"I thought I heard you had one of those."

"Yeah. Go on."

"They say you can have visions in those lodges. Well, I suppose I had one of those visions. It was very complicated, but it all boiled down to a strong vision of the power of the Divine. I suddenly found myself in the middle of a field, in an enormous thunderstorm. The lightning was striking everywhere, and with a force like I've never seen. Then something told me that this power was nothing compared to the Divine. I was then shown a glimpse of this divine power, not in itself, but as it exists in each person. You know, that life force inside us. I saw it, Grant. Pretty weird, huh? It was incredible. It was this mass of energy so intense and so enormous. It was brighter than the sun, radiating life and total energy! The power in each of us is incredible, Grant! Incredible." He sat up and held his thumb and forefinger together in front of my face. "That little speck of life force we think we have within us is really more like a nuclear explosion. It's more like a thousand times a nuclear explosion. And that's just what's coming into us. Imagine the Divine itself!" He was getting more excited as he talked. "That's a lot of power. But it's power for good, you know? Most of us are afraid

to recognize it. But it's in everyone, and you shouldn't fear it."
He shook his head and looked up in the air, blown away once
again by the recollection of this awesome experience.

I found Lachy's vision astonishing. It fit so well with the
message I had been picking up, not only with Dottie, but also
in Soweto. "You've got that right!" I replied. "That's exactly the
message I was getting while with Dottie. Don't be afraid of the
power. Raise up the rod. Run into the roar! Hoka hey!" Lachy
looked a bit perplexed, and I realized he couldn't know what I
was talking about. I just grinned.

He turned and looked back toward the little room off the
camp garage. I could see that he was in deep thought, trying to
understand this vision and its meaning for himself. I too drifted into silence, deep in thought. The idea of the magnitude of
the divine power was something I wanted to remember for my
own healing. It seemed to me that somewhere in the last few
months I had lost my faith in the divine power because of those
brushes with death. I knew I needed to get that faith back and
begin to trust again. But what about Lachy Brown? Was it a coincidence that we had both wanted to talk, and that he knew I
wanted to hear about flying? Was his vision of the power in each
of us related to the message I was receiving not to be afraid of it?
I had to press Lachy again, just to check my senses.

"Don't be afraid of the power. Is this message for you too?
Do you think?" I asked, looking for some spiritual connection.

He didn't even pause to think. "I know that's true. You're
right on, buddy," he replied with another smile. Then he seemed
to sink into some sort of deep thought. I could see that he was
mulling something over in his mind, perhaps something he
wanted to tell me.

"So, you think there's a connection between our experiences?" Lachy asked. "Do you think I'm the one you envisioned
who wanted to meet with you? I did, you know. Maybe we

were supposed to be working together—some grand plan?" He chuckled as if what he was asking was in jest, but at the same time he seemed intrigued by the idea, and almost eager for me to say yes.

"Well, if we are supposed to meet, and I have little doubt about that, then you must have something to offer me, and perhaps I have something to offer you." I didn't know what I was talking about, but I knew one thing. I needed something from Lachy Brown. There was something about Lachy that was simply causing my heart to burn with longing. I wanted to know him, love him, hug him, hit him, yell at him, and cry on his shoulder, all at the same time. I was magnetically drawn to him, like a little boy might feel toward a long-lost brother. "Yes, we are supposed to learn something from each other. That's what I think."

"Well, if that's true, what's the purpose?" he responded. "Why do you need to meet me? What do you need to know?"

"I don't know. I told you I've been shocked and frightened lately, and it's pretty cool that you are a pilot. Got any good stories about flying for me? Any good war stories about bravery?"

Hearing those words, Lachy looked up and stared off into the distance. He smiled and shook his head, and then frowned, and then smiled again. He was debating something. I could see that he was reaching back into his memory, and whatever it was he was accessing was bringing up some kind of issue—perhaps pain. He looked over at me again, with a certain resolve now in his eyes.

"So, you want to hear a story? I think I know the one I'm supposed to tell you. It happened in Vietnam." With those words Lachy launched into a story he said he hadn't told in a couple of decades. It was the story I was supposed to hear.

He began by explaining why he went to Vietnam, what it was like when he got there, how he became a Cobra helicopter pilot. He told me how his philosophy about the war changed during his stay, how he stopped writing home because it was too painful. He paused for a moment, and then looked at me with that same smile as before, as if he were holding something back that he knew he was supposed to share. Then his face changed slightly, with a sense of resolve.

"I don't tell this very often, but I think you would especially appreciate it." I sat up in anticipation. He launched into the story he had been so hesitant to tell.

It was February 15, 1970, Lachy's twenty-first birthday. He had been in Vietnam for a little more than one month. He was assigned to the 229th Assault Helicopter Battalion, 1st Cavalry Division. He was flying copilot in an AH-1G Cobra gunship with a cockpit that, he said, resembled a jet fighter. "It was very sleek and narrow, with the copilot seated in front of the pilot. It had lots of firing power. On this particular day we were called out on a mission to look for the pieces of a downed chopper in a very dangerous region of Nha Be, twenty miles south of Saigon.

"We were accompanying a small scout helicopter. The aircraft commander in the scout wanted to land and take a look at the wreck, and our job was to cover him from the air. We arrived at the area and didn't see anything out of the ordinary. The scout craft landed with the commander, pilot, and a tail gunner on board. But just as the commander jumped out of the helicopter, all hell broke loose. I could see the tracer fire of the enemy hitting the side of their aircraft. The door gunner in the back of the scout was killed immediately. A white phosphorus grenade went off in the back of the scout and an intense fire erupted. I don't know if a bullet set it off or what. The pilot still in the scout helicopter saw the commander on the ground drop and thought he had been killed. He gave the chopper full power to get out of there, not realizing that he was on fire. He got the helicopter up to about one hundred feet and then nose-dived into the ground. We were shooting rockets and the mini-gun all around the area."

"So they were all dead?"

"Hang on." He took another drag off of a newly-lit cigarette and proceeded with the story.

"As we came around the burning wreckage a second time, we figured no one could have survived the crash. I thought for certain that the pilot was dead. But then I saw the pilot crawl away from the burning wreckage. I was amazed. We were transmitting a Mayday call on the emergency band, giving our position and asking for help from any other helicopters in the area. But we also knew that we had to go down there and pull the guy out. As we were coming down shooting, we noticed that the scout commander was gone from where he had been lying. This meant that he was alive, and that there were now two pilots on the ground we had to get to. Since I was the new guy, and the copilot, I knew it was my job to jump out and try to locate both pilots. My senior pilot told me he would drop me and then go up and keep shooting rockets around the area while I located the two pilots."

"You must have been pretty scared."

He shook his head. "I didn't even think about it at that particular moment. You know, when you've gotta do what you've gotta do, you just do it. We landed very close to the hurt pilot. I jumped out and ran toward him as my gunship lifted off and began shooting. As I got to him, I saw that he was really badly burned by the fire. He was in shock and didn't seem to realize how badly he was hurt. The fire had eaten through his flight suit, and the nylon shoulder straps had melted to his collar. I was amazed that he was still on his feet. Just as we were getting ready to run for cover, I heard a noise like a bull moose going through the dry woods coming right at us from the other side of the clearing. Luckily I didn't shoot before I looked, because it was the aircraft commander from the scout. He came running toward us shouting, 'Let's go, I think they're right behind me!' So we ran blindly through the brush for about a hundred yards or more until we came to another clearing.

"At this point I realized that I had not brought a radio, and had no way to talk to the gunship. The only thing to do was step out into the clearing and hope he would see us. That was a really difficult thing to do. It was like setting yourself up as a sitting duck. I didn't want to go out there and expose myself, but I knew it was the only way for the helicopter to see us. I ran out and just stood there waiting for the Cobra pilot to fly over. It seemed like an eternity standing in that clearing, expecting to be shot at any time. Finally he came around very low and saw us. As he came hovering in, I knew the landing area was going to be tight. He was about ten feet above me when an RPG, that's a rocket propelled grenade, came from beyond the clearing, just missing the helicopter and hitting a large tree."

"No kidding!"

"No. They must have been waiting for him. The debris from the explosion flew into the tail rotor and the helicopter began to shake. I didn't know if the pilot noticed his tail rotor had been hit, so I waved him off. It was just too dangerous for him to try to come down and maneuver that thing in this small clearing without full control. The Cobra had to pull out. We found out later that he had to make an emergency landing about a mile away, where he found a large field.

"As the helicopter was leaving, we didn't stick around to see who had fired the RPG, we took off like three scared rabbits. While we were moving we began to hear other helicopters overhead. We knew they were looking for us. We ran about three hundred yards until we came to another clearing. I really didn't want to go stand in the middle again. It was like stepping into the lion's den. But standing in the open was the only way we would be seen. Again it seemed like forever until a Huey, which is a troop-carrying helicopter, came around from behind a tall stand of trees. As if in slow motion, I saw one of the crew members point at us. The helicopter banked into a tighter turn and lined up to land. At this point I realized that even though I felt like I was standing naked in the middle of Yankee Stadium, in fact the area where I was standing was too small to fit the helicopter in. The pilot could not land all the way because of the scrub brush and trees."

"Not again."

"Wait. He brought the Huey in close enough that he could safely hover with the skid about six feet above the ground. The other two pilots came running over. We grabbed the injured pilot and threw him into the hovering helicopter. Next, I made a cradle and the scout commander used it as a step to grab the skid and the doorpost of the helicopter and pull himself up. Then it was my turn. I grabbed the skid with one hand and realized that the helicopter was starting to lift. I knew I didn't have the strength to pull myself in. You don't know how terrifying and lonely that felt. I couldn't get up into the Huey. Only a few seconds passed, but it felt like forever. Then the flight commander reached down with his hand and latched on to my wrist." Lachy paused in wonder and delight. "Grant, it was the biggest hand I had ever seen! It was as big as a house! He gave a pull that launched me into the cabin of the helicopter. Without even stopping to explain, we both muscled the door gunners out of the way and started shooting the machine guns back over the area we had just come from."

"Man. That's incredible." I didn't know what else to say. I was just about speechless. Lachy finished the story by explaining that they made it safely back to base, and that he never did know whether the burned pilot survived or not. He ended by saying, "I guess that was a lucky twenty-first birthday, huh?"

My mouth was wide open at this point. Like a little boy, I simply said, "Wow." Here I heard a story far beyond anything I had hoped for, a story of such drama and intensity and even more bravery than I could have imagined. Somehow his every word gave me a bit more courage than I had before.

"Yeah. It was just the other day that I pulled out the old picture to take a look at it," he added nonchalantly.

"What picture?" I inquired.

"Well I had sort of put it away with the whole Vietnam experience. The picture of them pinning on the star."

"What star?"

"Oh. The Silver Star." He looked out into the woods and remained silent.

"The Silver Star? I didn't know that. You got the Silver Star for bravery?" I asked again in surprise.

"Yep. So that's the story," he said, still staring off into the woods.

I knew what Lachy meant when he said, "So that's the story." It was exactly what I needed to hear. I wondered at the fact that at this time I needed so much to talk to a slightly older and much wiser man, to teach me about courage and strength of character, and I had been led to a war hero. The words of Jesus kept repeating in my mind, "Greater love has no one than this, than to lay down one's life for his friends." Here's a guy who, at twenty-one years old, a kid, stepped into the roar to save someone else! I felt so close to Lachy while I listened to his words, as if I had known him all my life. I was so proud of him. He helped me so much that day with his words, his kindness, and his gentle strength of character.

I still wondered if I had that type of courage within me. I certainly didn't feel it. The fear was too great. In many ways I felt like I was looking for "the biggest hand I had ever seen" to come swoop me up and take me away from this dark jungle of dread I found myself trapped in. Maybe Lachy was offering that hand. I didn't know. One thing I did know, because my warming heart was telling me with every pulsating beat—I had found a big brother in Lachy Brown.

We talked for a few more minutes, but then, almost on cue, both of us got up to go our separate ways. We promised that we would talk again, if not at camp, then when we both returned home. Since he lived so close to my house, if we made the effort, we could talk again many times in the future. I knew we would.

14

A CIRCLE OF BROTHERS

As twilight descended on the wooded camp, we made preparations for our evening ritual for the teens. The men gathered the male teens in the lecture hall. Virtually every male in camp over thirteen years of age was there, from young to old, totaling about forty all together. The plan was to blindfold the young men and escort them down to an abandoned camp about a quarter mile outside main camp, where we would begin our honoring ceremony around a bonfire.

I could tell that the young men were ready for this new experience. They put on the usual air of nonchalance, but their jokes and clumsy interaction told me that they were excited. As the blindfolds were put over their eyes, they became silent, and the leader of our ceremonies followed this silence with the command, "From now on, there will be no talking of any kind until we reach our destination."

I glanced across the array of blindfolded boys and my eyes caught hold of Ronnie and Jason, who were standing next to each other, blindfolded and silent. Both extended their hands slightly forward into empty space, growing accustomed to their darkness. Something in my heart turned as I stared at them; a bit of sadness came over me. I didn't know what this was about, except that they looked so innocent and vulnerable, and perhaps I was too keenly aware of my children's vulnerability these days. But I was glad that they were taking part in this evening. I looked forward to all the men honoring them, and was glad that they were getting something I never had as a child. They would be accepted into the fellowship of older men, men who would be there in times of need, men who, tonight, would share their wisdom and extend their support.

The boys were systematically lined up behind one another, with their hands on the person's waist in front of them. The older men gathered around this line as escorts, and the signal was given to proceed with the march. As we made our way down the path that would take us over two walking bridges and through some dense woods, one man, Stan Morey, sounded a drum in the form of an intermittent heartbeat. *Boom, boom,* echoed into the valley; then there was silence. Just as the echo faded, another heartbeat sounded. *Boom, boom.* The contrast between the intermittent drumming and the silence of the blinded marchers projected a surreal atmosphere over all of us. It was otherworldly, timeless.

When we reached a point where we could see the distant fire burning, we halted the group of teens. The older men then arranged themselves in two facing lines to form a human tunnel through which the boys would pass. One by one, the young men were sent blindfolded through the tunnel on their final journey to the fire. As each boy passed through our gauntlet, a man would reach out and touch his shoulder and say a word of encouragement. I had given the older men a few suggestions of what they might say, and as the boys passed through I heard a variety of these messages of honor and support.

"Aho, friend."

"The Lord be with you."

"May you have peace."

"Ho."

"Bless you."

"Welcome, friend."

"The Lord be with you."

I wondered what it must have been like to be one of those young men, receiving a touch of masculine love and the gentle words of support from older men. It must have been powerful. I reflected with a deep joy that even though this type of ceremony might be looked upon by some as pretty "out there," it was incredibly special and so useful. *If only every young man had this opportunity,* I thought to myself. *How much easier their lives would be! How much more tolerable the pain!* When I was a boy I longed so much for the support of an older man. My father loved me, I had no doubt, but he didn't show it physically or talk about it verbally. Besides this, I had no older brother to teach me, to wrestle with me, or even to beat me up. It was a lonely, empty childhood. I had to be my own mentor, as many men my age did. We tried to rely on each other during our youth in the sixties and seventies. We suffered through our bad choices and blunders. Who could blame us? It was the blind leading the blind. But we watched out for each other, and we survived. I know I promised myself that this would not happen to my children. They would have a mentor to watch out for them, to help them in good and bad times, to help them grow. Hopefully they would know many older men in the community, and would feel free to go to them for wisdom or for help. What was happening this night was part of this hope and dream.

As the last boy traveled through our gauntlet, we gathered

them in a circle around the fire, placing an older man between each of the younger ones, and removed their blindfolds. The drum ceased. The boys rubbed their eyes, gazing at the fire, the woods, the sky above the trees, and their brothers around them. In silence, the leaders lit two large sticks of sage and walked around the circle, blowing the sweet smoke around everyone's bodies.

"This is for protection," the leader of the ceremony said. "Native Americans believed that the sage would ward off evil spirits. The smoke can be a symbol of our oneness and a sphere of love and support as we share our hearts tonight." Everyone sat down together on the grass, creating a circle around the fire. I could see the others' faces dimly lit by the firelight. It was my turn to speak.

"We are here as men to honor one another, and to honor men who have made a difference in our lives," I explained to them. "I am holding a stick in my hand. It is a talking stick. The one who holds this stick is the only one who may talk. In a moment we will pass the stick to each man. When you receive it, speak from the heart, not from the head. Each man here will have an opportunity to talk about some man who has made a difference in his life. You may pass. And remember, there are forty of us here, so don't go on too long, or we'll be here all night."

A muffled laugh went up from the crowd. And in the break of laughter a hand reached out from behind me and grabbed the talking stick from my hands. I turned to see Lachy Brown standing in the firelight, stick in hand, with a look of command and purpose as a very light wind blew on his hair.

"Wait a minute! We've forgotten something here," he abruptly interjected. "Let's not forget those men who couldn't be here in person tonight but who are with us in spirit. This is another custom of great importance to the Native Americans.

Let us honor the men that are with us from the spirit world, our wise elders who have gone before us—our fathers, grand-fathers, brothers, and sons. They too are here to share their presence. Let us not forget them." He handed the stick back to me and sat down.

A few men made verbal acknowledgment of his words.

"Ho!"

"Yes."

"We honor them."

I was taken aback by his interruption. I was aware that this honoring of the elders who had gone into the afterlife was a custom of the Native Americans, but I didn't plan to use it. It seemed inappropriate to me to honor ghosts and spirits and such in a church setting. Besides, I had enough trouble with them growing up. I didn't want any ghosts summoned here to hang around, especially the one I had been running from. I was miffed that he would just interrupt and inject something unplanned into the program. But as I fumbled with the stick, trying to gather my thoughts, I looked around and recognized from their faces and comments that the men felt this was very useful. Perhaps many of the men we would speak about as hav-ing made a difference in our lives were on the other side now, fathers, grandfathers, and others. But Lachy could have asked me first. I gathered myself and let my brief moment of resent-ment pass in acknowledgment that what Lachy suggested was probably a good thing. Maybe those loved ones of another world would be with us tonight. Maybe they'd take heart in the honoring.

I began the sharing. As the leader of this process, it was my job to start it off by modeling the type of sharing one might do. It was hard to get in touch with my feelings. I began by shar-ing something about my father. "My father is a gentle man. He didn't have to be that way. My father and his twin brother were treated very badly by my grandfather. He used to take them to the Atlantic City boardwalk when they were eight years old. Sounds good, doesn't it? You might imagine him buying them cotton candy, and treating them to the Ferris wheel and other rides. But this isn't what happened." I began to feel pressure behind my eyes as they became wet. "He took them there every weekend, set up a boxing ring in the middle of the boardwalk, and made them box each other for people's entertainment." I paused for a moment and then continued, "He made them fight for money that went into his pocket. They'd fight till they were bloody, or their old man would beat them with a belt when they got home. Dad says that sometimes he would just beat them for no reason at all, for what he called 'good measure.'

"If someone tried to do something like that with his kids today, he'd be arrested. My dad could have grown up with that same cruelty and self-interest. But he didn't. He's a quiet man, and doesn't say a lot to me. He never gets too deep. He likes to talk about business, and sports, not much more than that. But life wasn't easy for him—not even as an adult. As a young father he lost his only son. His little boy died alone in a hospital bed. How sickening and hard that must have been for my father! I can't imagine living if I lost one of my sons. Yet my father carried on, and when I came along years later, he treated me as if I was the only one, his only son. He gave me everything I ever needed. He taught me so many things. Though he never said it, his actions showed me that he loved me. I am grateful, and I honor him for these things." I finished, wiped my face, and passed the stick to the next man.

I don't remember much of what the next few men said, because I was in deep thought about my father. He was such a strong man, and in business he had done well. He was generous with his help, especially when Cathy and I were married while still in college. But I often thought that this man's quiet nature hid the real grief and sadness within his heart. I could never get him to talk about it. He didn't seem to want to talk of sad things, but rather live for today and provide for tomorrow.

Focusing back on the process at hand, I heard men and boys speaking with open hearts, and often from a place of pain. There was a lot of pain shared that night, and also gratitude in those faces, as each spoke of a man who had made a difference to him in his life. There was a lot of love in those voices. Some of the boys' comments were especially meaningful. Several spoke of their fathers, some of whom were not at camp with their children. One spoke of how his father worked hard to keep the family afloat, and how much he loved his father, though his father probably didn't know it. Others spoke of friends who were present and thanked them for their brotherhood and companionship.

As the stick moved around the circle, it came to Jason. He spoke in a matter-of-fact way, with a bit of embarrassment, but his words brought me comfort and a sweet sense of peace and happiness.

"I'd like to honor my dad," he said. "He's done a lot for me. He's taught me everything I know. And he's not your typical minister type. He's pretty cool. I mean, he listens to me, and he believes in me. I know that's not always true with dads. So I honor my dad." Jason finished speaking and passed the stick to his older brother. I couldn't see Jason's face because he was sitting directly on the other side of the fire from me, but I could sense the smile within his calm words. He was so mature and thoughtful for a thirteen-year-old. He had a strong spiritual sense about him too. I often wondered whether he would become a minister. I was touched by his words. As he finished, I found a few tears rolling down my cheeks, as if he had begun some breaking down process on what was left of the emotional armor surrounding my heart.

Ronnie went next, and spoke very slowly and tenderly. "I want to honor a man, a leader of men, a healer, a spiritual warrior. He has taught me everything I know. He has taught me the ways of wisdom. He is a great man. He is my father." His voice broke as he finished and passed the stick along. And as his voice broke, mine broke out in a cry of emotion. The process Jason had started within me, Ronnie had finished. The armor dropped away from my heart, emotions were freely released, and I buried my head in my lap to hide my weeping. It lasted a few minutes as others spoke. I had tried so hard to raise my boys to be good men, honest, sincere, spiritual. I didn't know that they had noticed. I didn't know that in my personal fight to break down the barriers to love that so many people set up, and to bring a little more love and understanding to the world, that my sons were watching, and understanding not only what I was doing, but who I was as a man. I was so grateful to have this time in the firelight, in the woods of western Pennsylvania, to hear their voices of gratitude and love. We had all been through so much recently. My sons were alive, not only on a physical level, but in their spirits as well. What more could a father ask? Ronnie's and Jason's words were imprinted on my heart that night, never to fade.

As the stick had just about made its journey around the circle, it was close to midnight. One of the other two ministers who were at camp this particular week took the stick and began to speak. His name was Jeremy. Jeremy was usually a very cheerful fellow with a lot of wit. He was the kind of man that you wouldn't expect to cry, and he wasn't crying as he spoke, at least outwardly. But his words bespoke his grief within as well as his pride.

"I want to honor someone many of you younger ones don't know." Jeremy spoke in a low, contemplative voice. "Lachy spoke of honoring those who are here with us from the other side. I want to speak about one of these. I have a brother. His name is Rick. He was a hero in Vietnam. He received the Silver Star for his act of heroism, though he never saw it. You see, my brother Rick, he and his platoon were caught in a firefight one night. His platoon was torn to shreds. He managed to crawl out of it, but his buddies were wounded and left behind. Well, Rick went back into the firefight and dragged each one of his wounded buddies out of there to safety. He would bring one out at a time and then go in to get another. It was the last one . . . There was one more he went back for . . ." Jeremy paused and gathered himself. "He was killed trying to save the last man." He paused again in the darkness, the fire beginning to burn out in the night. "My brother received the Silver Star at his funeral. I haven't thought about him in a long time. Maybe he's here tonight."

When Jeremy finished, the men sat silently, in a hush, touched by his words. In the quiet, I reflected. I had known Jeremy had a brother who had died in the Vietnam War. And I wondered that I had heard two stories of war heroes that day. I certainly felt for Jeremy, losing his big brother like that. I thought of Bruce. I wondered, if he had lived, whether he would have gone to that war. Would he have been friends with Lachy and Rick? He would have been about the right age.

As some men gazed into the fire and others up into the stars above the trees, I could sense that there were a lot of brothers hanging around that fire at that moment, brothers from every world and generation. A silent salute from all of us ascended into the sky for Jeremy's brother, Rick, and others like him. As we gathered our things and stomped out the fire in preparation for leaving that most sacred place, I thanked God for this evening. I hugged and congratulated the men who had helped plan the event, and thanked them for having the courage to stand up for this process. I turned one more time to gaze upon this sacred space we were now leaving. I saw Lachy Brown with his arm around Jeremy, as one brother comforting another. Lachy had been to Vietnam. Lachy wore the Silver Star. Lachy knew Rick. Both of these men had run into the roar to save another human being. But one brother in arms had made it, and the other had passed too early to the other side. Both heroes, one continued to walk this earth, while the other treaded fields of another land, another kind of world. That night they were all there, reunited in memory and in love.

The following day was our last in the camp. Just before beginning the task of packing up our belongings, cleaning out the cabin, and saying our goodbyes to other campers, I leaned against an old oak tree, lit up my pipe, and reflected upon the week. It had certainly been meaningful. I had received so much. I felt grateful for my sharing group, who so sincerely listened to my story and offered their gentle words. I would cherish the memory of the men's gathering the night before, for what my sons had said and for that image of Lachy comforting Jeremy. I gained a new friend in Lachy—more than a friend, a brother. And the wild spiritual experience with Dottie—spiritual wars, messages of love from whispering angels, healing! It certainly made life interesting, though I wasn't exactly sure what I was supposed to make of it all.

Cathy and I had been so busy that we hadn't had much time to connect. But this was typical of such camps, and we'd have plenty of time to catch up with each other in Wisconsin. I wanted to tell her about the night with the men and what our boys had said. Cathy was truly the grounded half of our relationship. She'd listen and believe what I said, but she was good at keeping me from flying off into outer space. In fact, I looked forward to talking to her in depth about my otherworldly experience. It seemed so real when I was with Dottie, and at least viable while talking to Lachy. But, as I leaned on that tree and watched the camp being slowly disassembled as people packed to go home, the thought came to me that perhaps this particular spiritual experience should also be disassembled and packed away. It was just too far-out, and it probably was a result of my recent emotional breakdown.

Having finished my pipe, I noticed Lachy and a woman from our group coming down the path past our cabin. As he approached, I realized that this would be my last chance to debrief about our conversation, at least for a few weeks. The thought occurred to me that maybe Lachy was just a nice guy who wouldn't dare confront me about my lunacy. Maybe he was simply being polite when I told him about the spiritual experience with Dottie. On the spur of the moment, I decided to take the opportunity to minimize what I had told him this week. As he passed by with a smile and a nod, I grabbed his arm.

"Hey, Lachy, can I talk to you for a minute?" He stopped and looked concerned for me. I immediately assumed that he must be worried that I was going to go on another verbal tirade.

"Sure, Grant. What's up?" he asked.

"You know all that stuff we were talking about the other day?"

"Yeah?"

"Well, I just want you to know that this really could have been just some sort of hallucination or maybe just some peculiar occurrence with no basis. I mean, it might not mean anything. Now that we're headed back to the real world, I just want you to know that I'm usually not that strange, really! Why don't you just forget about that stuff I told you?"

"What do you mean?" He looked mildly confused.

"What I mean is that all that spiritual stuff is a bunch of crap. Forget about it."

Lachy's face turned intense, almost angry. Then his intensity broke, and he smiled a very devilish grin through that half-grown beard. He grabbed my arm and yanked me a few feet away from the cabins. He put his face close to my ear and whispered, "Listen, if you were new to this war I might understand why you're recanting, but you're not, soldier! Stand your ground!" With that, he let go of me and walked into the cabin. I chuckled at his words and my own lack of faith. I had received a big-brother scolding, and it was just what I needed. I looked forward to meeting up with Lachy again once we returned home from vacation.

Our family said goodbye to all in the camp, closed the car doors, and headed down the road toward Wisconsin. As we hit the Pennsylvania Turnpike and headed toward Ohio and beyond, my heart was full of gratitude and my mind of so many images and loving memories of this week at camp. I turned to the boys in the backseat and said, "Hey, you want to hear a good story? It's about a real war hero. You know him. His name is Lachy Brown."

PART 4

ENCHANTED
FOREST

15

THE NORTHWOODS

The ride to Wisconsin went by quickly. Cathy and I had much catching up to do, and the four boys had plenty of stories to share with each other. I had told her bits and pieces about Lachy Brown and my time with Dottie, but as we drove toward the solitude of the Northwoods, I filled her in completely. I also told her about the men's gathering and Jeremy's story. She shared her experience with the gathering of women. She was also interested to know more about my feelings of dread and how they fared over the week. She had said earlier that she had pretty well recovered from the close call on the plane and even from Steven's accident, but now she was feeling it again.

"Grant, what are your feelings about the accident? Do you think Lachy and Dottie helped you out? I know I had some good time to talk about the whole thing with people at camp, but I need this vacation in a bad way. I don't ever want to see a SEPTA bus again. There aren't any buses in the Northwoods, right?" she joked.

"No, no buses, just bears, lakes, and dark forests. Maybe we could just lock Steven up for the next two weeks," I replied in my usual sarcastic manner.

"Shhhhh! He'll hear you. He's tired of hearing about it. He doesn't even remember it. I know it's hard, but we're just going to have to let go of it and trust. You can't make yourself crazy worrying about your children's safety at every turn. It was a freak accident. Right? I know those close calls with death brought up a lot of childhood fears in you. I've been thinking about my childhood too, about my father's death. I guess thinking about us being killed and leaving the kids behind brought back his death for me. I was in the dark about the whole thing, being only eight years old. I used to dream he came home, but then I'd wake up and realize that he was still gone. I don't want that to happen to my children."

"It must have been tough on your mother, with six kids and all. Your mom doesn't talk about it much either, does she?" I asked.

"No. I've asked her about it, and she'll talk when I ask. But she doesn't say that much." Cathy sighed.

"Well, apparently it's very hard to talk about these things. That older generation just doesn't talk like ours does. Maybe we talk too much." I thought of my mother's sad silence. "I wonder what my mother used to dream about her son?"

"What do you mean?" Cathy asked.

"I mean about Steven."

"You mean Bruce!" Cathy sternly replied.

"Damn it!" I hit the steering wheel with the palm of my hand, angry at myself for the mistake. "I did it again!"

"That's the second time."

"No, it's the third time," I replied. "I did it in my group this week."

"You're kidding!"

"No, I'm serious. What do you think that's about? I just don't get it. It's obvious that Bruce's death and Steven's accident are related somehow in my unconscious mind. It's obviously some core childhood issue having to do with my own fears."

"Do you think you're mixing them up because Bruce died as a child, and now that Steven's come so close to death you're lumping them together or something?" Cathy asked, grasping for the right words.

"I guess. Bruce died at age two, though, and Steven's nine. But I do think of them in the same way—as, I don't know, young, vulnerable little boys. You know, I've never thought about Bruce so much since this incident. Maybe I've been jarred into fears that my son will die because my parents' son died. If it's true that my mother always put that fear into me, it would make sense. Does that make sense?" I squinted my eyes in puzzlement.

"You mean you're afraid Steven will die because Bruce did?" she asked.

"I suppose. I don't know. Something's missing in all of this."

"What about your own fear of dying? Is that related?"

"Well, wouldn't that make sense too? I mean, I grew up with that fear, though I didn't know where it came from. It was almost like every time I got sick my mother would say, 'Oh no, my little boy is going to die! My little boy is going to die because . . .' She would never finish the sentence. She never said why. It was just a big scary mystery at the time. I didn't even know she had another son who died."

"How did you find out?"

"Well, it's not like they hid it from me. They just never talked about it. I'm sure they thought about him every day, but they never said a word or acknowledged him in any way. I remember Mom kept a small photo of him on her shelf in her room. And

I discovered a few photos of him once in her drawer. He was standing in a baby pool with this distant, concerned look on his face. I asked her who it was. She told me it was baby Bruce, who died before I was born. I think I was probably only seven or eight years old at the time. I just said, 'Oh.' And that was the end of our conversation and my knowledge about Bruce. I don't remember how I found out the way he died. I didn't even know about them going home from the hospital and then being called back until last month. Cathy, he just wasn't a reality in our family. Pretty strange, huh?"

"Well, we didn't talk about Daddy too much either. I guess it was just too painful.... Sometimes, though, besides the dreams as a child, I did get a sense of my father's presence. It only happened a few times, but it felt very real.... I don't know. Some of that might be wishful thinking. Do you ever think you sense your brother's presence?" she asked.

I thought about it. I couldn't think of any time I had felt his presence, though I remembered a similar conversation I once had with my cousin Terry Schnarr, who was also a minister. "I have talked about that with Terry, and how maybe Bruce's being on the other side may have pulled us away from our 'evil' family tendencies. We used to joke that my grandfather rolled over in his grave when we became ministers. I mean, you know, *schnarr* means 'disturber of the peace' in German. Schnarrs are known for drunken brawls and all that. My grandfather was so bad he used to have a picture of his girlfriend on his dresser. My grandmother never said a thing."

"Talk about codependency!" Cathy observed.

"Yeah, you've got that right!" I continued. "So when Terry and I bucked the system and became ministers it was a shock to the whole family. It was Terry who said that Bruce was probably responsible for that. He said that since Bruce went to the other side to become an angel, he kind of balanced things up in the other world. Terry said he often thinks of Bruce as being the guardian angel who gives both of us support. I guess I had thought about it, but I never felt it. Bruce was only two years old when he died. He's off playing in some celestial sandbox right now, as far away from me as, I guess, as God is."

"You think of God as far away? Grant. You have a good sense of God in your life. I mean, think about those times when God seemed so close. And isn't your whole personal mission to help people feel God's presence?"

"I guess I thought I had a good connection with God, though recently he's seemed pretty far away. I don't know. But Bruce? Bruce is up there enjoying his celestial bliss, unaware that he has a brother down here struggling to make sense of life. He couldn't care less about me. Sometimes I feel that way about God too. I mean, where is God? What's he done for us lately, except to scare the crap out of us?"

"You seem angry."

"I suppose. Maybe I'm just tired."

Toward evening we rolled through the hills of northern Wisconsin. I felt refreshed by the clean air and smell of the pines all around. Yet I still sensed that the fears had not left me. As we drove down the two-lane road leading toward our cabin in the woods, I pretended that I was flying a DC-10, moving the steering wheel with care, absorbing the turbulence as we bounced on the road. I recognized that the road was bumpier than any turbulence I had ever encountered before. Why was I so afraid to fly? The little game passed the time as we drove in silence toward our destination.

As I continued to captain my "airplane" I thought about the conversation earlier with Cathy. Cathy and I had wanted a break from all this focus on death and loss, and yet that's just about all we ended up talking about on this trip. While it was painful, I had a sense that it was part of the healing process. The conversation gave me some things to think about. I wondered, for instance, whether Bruce was around me. I certainly didn't sense it. But in many ways my life did seem charmed, and I wondered whether his guardianship as an angel hadn't played a part in this. I reflected that every time I needed money for something it seemed to show up, that I had encountered some good success in starting my own church, and that the people who rallied around me seemed to really like me. I had even gotten a few books and pamphlets published, and our family had its fifteen minutes of fame on the national television show *America's Funniest People,* winning the $10,000 prize! Somebody was watching over me. I had always given the credit for my good fortune to God, who no doubt deserved it, but I was always taught that God doesn't work in a vacuum. He works through his angels.

How ironic! I thought to myself. I considered my life a charmed one indeed, but here I cowered in fear of death itself. Here I wondered whether there was any God in my life who could care for me and my family in this dangerous world! *Wow, I am such an emotional mess!*

A few minutes later, as we began to get closer to our cabin in Hazelhurst, Cathy and I talked about how this would probably be the last year we'd come here, at least for a while. Though the trip was shorter from Laurel Hill, it was a nineteen-hour drive from our home. It was just too much to do every year. However, this year was special. The boys' club our sons belonged to when we lived in Chicago was holding its camp during the second week of our vacation, and it was only three hours south of our cabin. The plan was to drop off our sons next week so that they could be with their friends at camp. Cathy and I would be alone for some real relaxation.

When we turned down the little road leading to our cabin on the lake, the rich forest enveloped us. The cedars and oaks rocketed up into the sky above us, and the gentle wind moved the foliage just enough to make the forest seem alive. As we pulled into the driveway and stopped beside our cabin, the lake glistening in the setting sun before us and a loon calling in the distance, Cathy turned to me with a smile.

"Maybe we should come back next year."

"Yeah, we definitely want to come back next year." The place was just too irresistible: compelling, magnetic in its beauty, thick with a spiritual aura. But the most inspiring and even healing aspect of this land was its peace. Hazelhurst was called "the quiet side of the Northwoods" by the local residents. Most nights were so still that it took me a few nights before I could fall asleep easily, being used to the sound of cars driving by the house at home and the usual noises of suburbia. The silence here was deafening, except for the occasional call of the loon out on the water.

The whole family unpacked the car and settled into the cabin just before dark. On one of my trips between the car and the cabin, I stopped on the path leading to the house and breathed in the fresh Northwoods air, listening to the silence. I could feel it penetrating me, easing my tense body and hushing my anxieties. As we unpacked the last of our supplies I stepped out onto the porch to sit and reflect for a while. Such peace! Such quietness and serenity!

Just as I began to relax, I heard the sound of a guitar plug being inserted into a very powerful amplifier and a snare drum beat a quick roll. Then someone began to play a bass guitar. Suddenly, the Northwoods were invaded by the loudest punk rock music I had ever heard, even from Ronnie's and Jason's stereo. The neighbors down the way were having a band party. The quieter side of the Northwoods transformed into Woodstock '96!

"What on earth is that?" Cathy shouted from the kitchen.

"I guess it's the neighbor. Can you believe this? In all my years up here I've never heard anything like this! This is crazy!"

I was upset. Didn't they know that this was a haven for people escaping this kind of noise? How dare they do this?

Ronnie walked onto the porch to join me. "Well, maybe if they were any good, it might be tolerable. But these guys suck!" I had to agree. The bass player was at least a measure behind the rhythm guitar player, and the lead guitarist played nonstop related melodies while the singer, or maybe should I say "shouter," tried to yell over the entire din. Then it really got bad. The singer launched into a series of profanities. This was the last straw.

"Why don't you go over there and tell them to turn it down?" Cathy suggested as she joined us on the porch. I knew she was going to ask me that.

"Listen, I don't want to do that. Maybe one of the neighbors will. Why don't we wait a while?" I really hated confrontation, especially with strangers. The fear of doing something like that was just too great. "OK, I know. I'm a coward."

"Maybe Ronnie or Jason would go over." Cathy was now baiting me. If they could do it, why couldn't I?

"Jason and Owen are already over there listening to the band," Ronnie informed us with a typical teenage roguish grin.

"You've got to be kidding."

"No, they left as soon as the music started."

"Why don't you go over, Ronnie?" Cathy shot back.

"Hey, I'm with Dad. Those guys will stop soon. Somebody will tell them to turn it down." He had more confidence than the other boys in handling his mother's requests. He smiled and waltzed back to the boys' room to strum his own acoustic guitar.

We sat and tried to relax as the music continued at the same volume for another hour. Jason and Owen returned home to tell us, "It was a really big crowd, but the band wasn't that good."

"I'm calling the police," Cathy said with determination.

She looked up the phone number and called. I couldn't hear her conversation because I was outside listening to the music, but after about a minute the music stopped.

"If you haven't noticed, the music stopped, Cathy," I reported as I walked into the kitchen.

"Oh, the music stopped," Cathy informed the person on the other end of the phone. "How about I'll call you if it starts again? OK, OK, thanks. Bye." She turned to me with a look of amusement. "Did you know that the closest police department is thirty miles south of here? It would take them about an hour to get here."

"I didn't know that. I guess they don't need many policemen around here. But we don't need them anyway, now that the music's over," I replied.

"Well, they said they were willing to send a car along if it continued. I told them I'd call back if it started up again."

"Good. Well, it is after eleven. They're probably finished." We sent the two younger boys to bed and then headed off to bed ourselves. I had brought some outdoor adventure books by Tom Brown, and I was looking forward to some good quiet time for reading and reflection. I heard he was a very spiritual man, and a tracker at that. It sounded interesting.

No sooner had I opened the book and begun to read than the pounding of the drums and the wail of the guitars sounded again in loud unison. From the bedroom window I could hear the music bouncing off the trees on the other side of the lake, creating an echo with a four- or five-second delay. That made it sound even worse. I looked over at Cathy.

"Forget it. You call them," she said.

"Well, they'll stop sometime," I replied, and went back to my book. I read for a few minutes and then put the book down and fell asleep.

At 1:30 a.m. I awoke to silence. I don't remember whether

I had been dreaming or not, but I felt deeply disturbed. Cathy was sound asleep beside me. I climbed out of bed and looked out the window of our room. I couldn't see a thing. It was totally dark, not a light to be seen, not even from the moon or stars above, which were either blocked by the trees or obstructed by clouds. It was hot and the room seemed stuffy. I walked into the hall and looked into the boys' room next door. The two older ones were sprawled out onto their beds while the two younger ones slept neatly and quietly in sleeping bags on the floor.

Nothing wrong here, I thought to myself. Something felt wrong. Maybe it was simply the adjustment to being in a new and quiet place. I didn't know. As I walked into the kitchen, I looked out the door toward our car. I couldn't see it. It was too dark. Looking out all the windows filled me with dread. To see nothing but darkness out the window was too much for me, and the silence frightened me. I drank a glass of water and went back to bed.

16

LOVE AND FEAR

❦

The following few days at Hazelhurst were filled with fishing, walking, swimming, reading, and just lying around. The fishing was especially good that August, because it had been an unusually cool summer and the fish were still feeding near the surface. One of our favorite spots was a lake just north of ours that had been formed by a beaver dam. It was called Mud Lake. The four boys and I would paddle through a very narrow, winding stream to reach this treasure trove of fish. Once inside the small cove that surrounded the pond, we couldn't see any signs of civilization.

All that could be seen on every side was dense forest, a few rocky hills, a wild field, and birds and animals here and there. A blue heron often fished on the shore there. She would stand majestically and patiently in the shallow water, waiting for her food to swim by. Her long, thin legs and body always gave me the impression of a prehistoric bird. Her presence helped us to feel as if we were fishing back in time, before civilization as we know it.

"Let's pretend we're living like the Indians, Dad," Steven announced, his adventurous spirit mixed with a little wonder. "Do you think it looked like this when the Indians were here?"

"I do. And I think that's what makes this land so special. You can sense the spirit of the Indians here. It's very peaceful." In fact, sometimes the spirit of the Indians was so thick you could cut it with a tomahawk. Not only was the forest alive with a thick spiritual aura, every tree seemed to tell a story as its leaves rustled in the wind; every bird communicated more than a melody in its song. Even the lake itself seemed to have its own spirit that changed with the weather, from serene to troublesome, from jubilant to sad stillness. Cathy and I experienced this land as having dignity mixed with sadness.

This sense of sadness was especially acute on one particular peninsula on the lake called Szantay's Point. It was an uninhabited part of the lake with the ruins of what looked like the beginnings of a dream house overlooking the water. A short stone wall ran around the perimeter of the peninsula, and there was a dock down by the water, but no people—ever. It was a magical place, but so sad. During a gentle rain it sometimes seemed the peninsula itself would be weeping. Legend had it that a ghost dwelled there. Cathy and I found out the hard way.

Late one evening several years earlier we had put the children to bed and had gone down to the side of the lake for a little romance. A mist was forming on the water, and it was a beautiful, peaceful night. As we rolled out a mattress under the stars and laid down, we heard an incredibly eerie moan roll over the water from the other side of the lake. It was coming from Szantay's Point. It was loud, and it sounded part human and part I don't know what. It reminded me of the kind of moan we'd hear a ghost make on the old cartoon *Scooby Doo*. We sat up and strained our eyes to see if there were any lights coming from over at Szantay's Point, or signs of movement, but there were none. It was so strange and disturbing that we decided to continue our romantic evening up at the cabin.

It was a day or two later that I was reading an old history of Hazelhurst, and I came to a very interesting story about "The Ghost of Hazelhurst." A French fur trader had apparently taken an Indian bride here a hundred years ago. The local Indians didn't like this too much. In fact, the bride's first husband was sort of upset. So he took the fur trader out for a midnight cruise and hit him over the head and dropped him into the lake. The story went on to say, "And it is said that some nights in August, when a mist appears out on the lake, you can hear the fur trader mournfully crying for his life, out on the southern point [Szantay's Point]." Whether we heard that ghost or not that particular night, it makes for a good story.

Despite the ghost stories, the thick spiritual aura surrounding our lake brought more comfort and peace than fear. The place was alive with spirit, and one could easily lose any sense of time, commitments, or deadlines while paddling in the different waterways and lagoons. In many ways, the place seemed timeless. The boys and I paddled around in our rowboat, casting our rods into various locations, hoping for a big catch. We talked about what it must have been like to live in the wild, well before civilization appeared as we now know it. As the fish stole the bait off the boys' hooks one by one, the usual begging took place. "Dad, will you worm my hook?"

"No. You're all old enough to worm your own hooks now. For years you did all the fishing while I sat here and wormed hooks. Now it's my turn to fish. Worm your own hook!"

This response did not stop them from asking. They knew too well that continual badgering could wear me down. But I remained steadfast. Finally, after about twenty minutes, the fish started biting worm, hook, and all.

"I've got one!" Jason shouted. "Get out of my way, Owen! I can't bring it in!"

"Reel it in slowly, Jason, you'll lose it, stupid!" Owen replied.

The fish was a mid-sized lake bass. Jason wheeled his rod into the boat and the fish flapped on the floor before me.

"Wow. That's the biggest one today!" Jason pulled back on the rod, hoisting the fish near enough for him to unhook it. I half expected him to ask me to unhook it. But Jason was the only son who didn't mind worming hooks and unhooking fish.

"Can we cook this one? It looks big enough, don't you think? We haven't kept a fish all week. We should at least cook one." The hunter in Jason wanted fulfillment. It wasn't enough to just catch the fish. He had to take it home and complete the hunt by eating it.

"I just don't feel like killing any fish this week. If you want to kill and clean it then you can keep it. It's a lot of work for a few bites." I loved fishing but cleaning them for such little meat seemed like too much messy work. Besides, I wasn't into killing anything lately.

Jason offered to clean it at first, but after some thought he decided that the best thing to do would be to put it in a bucket and transport it over to the water near our dock. So we kept it in the bucket until we returned to the cabin, where the fish was released to new waters and a new lease on life. That week we caught a lot of fish, none bigger than Jason's, and we threw them all back into the water.

The time with my sons, fishing, talking, and playing together, was some of the best time of my life. With my heightened awareness of the frailty of life I drank in every moment of it. Their faces shining in the setting sun, their hair blowing in the wind, their laughter, their spirit of adventure filled me with gladness, and with such gratitude to have them as my sons. I don't know if I was still taking mental photos of them anymore. It was more like mental video at this point, which somehow gave me the impression that I must be getting better. The initial shock of our mishaps was slowly fading, but it would take time to feel "normal" again, whatever that word "normal" is supposed to mean.

On one early evening, as the sun was setting, the whole family jumped in our little outboard fishing boat and took a twilight cruise around the entire lake. It covered several square miles with a few lagoons, cabins scattered here and there, and a lot of open wilderness. As we passed by Szantay's Point, an eagle flew out from one of the tall cedars above us. His huge wings spread wide as he gently soared over our heads. Eagles were returning to the Northwoods, and it was an emotional experience to see it. We sat still in our little boat and watched this magnificent creature ascend above us.

"Look at that eagle! It's amazing!" Steven shouted as he pointed up toward it.

"Yes, they're returning to this land," I responded.

"You know, you're really lucky to see an eagle. Most people don't get to see these great birds. They're very rare," Cathy added.

Seeing the excitement on our sons' faces made me reflect on just how lucky they were. Not many boys would live to see the majesty of a real eagle in flight, and so close. My sons had so much going for them, not only the beauty of a place like this to return to each year, but they also had each other. Their friendship was so deep and so strong. Certainly they fought. They fought a lot about all sorts of things, but they also talked, played, explored, and lived together. They loved each other as only brothers could. As they grew older, I could see that they were spreading out their wings like eagles, learning to fly. Their childlike innocence was not so much fading, but being filled each day with an eagerness to take on the world, to soar high and far, to prepare for a life of their own. But they would never be alone. They had each other, and they had parents who cared and who would love them each new day of their lives.

As the eagle gained altitude above us, it circled our heads. I wondered, as was typical nowadays, whether this wasn't some sort of sign from above. Was this a statement from the Divine that we were being cared for, that God was watching over us, that we could find refuge under the shelter of his wings? But this thought soon vanished. The eagle turned, and then suddenly dove directly toward our little boat.

"What's happening?" Ronnie called out.

The eagle continued its dive-bomb toward us.

"I don't know. He's coming right at us!" Cathy exclaimed.

The eagle was, indeed, coming right at us, and for a brief moment I thought maybe he had mistaken us for some very large prey. As his huge wings passed over our heads, his claws descended into the water a few feet away next to the shoreline, and almost as quickly as he hit the water he was off again, heading toward the trees.

"Look, he was after one of those ducks!" Owen called out with excited amusement. Right at the shoreline swam a family of ducks, who were now stirred up and quacking away after the eagle's attack.

"He didn't get one, did he?" Cathy asked with motherly concern.

"No. He left empty-handed," I responded.

"Wow, that was cool!" Jason shouted. The boys all agreed.

"Well, you see, eagles are predators. They hunt for a living." I pretended to give the boys a little nature lesson, but I was really clandestinely attempting to calm Cathy down.

"Yes, but those poor little ducks! Are you sure he didn't get one?" Cathy asked again.

"He didn't get one." I tried to offer consolation. "But if he did, I mean, that's what eagles do!"

"Well, that was pretty amazing! I wonder if he'll try again." Ronnie asked as he looked upward into the trees, searching for a sign of the large bird's presence. We all searched the trees and sky. The bird was gone.

The eagle passing right over our heads was an incredible experience. We could have almost reached out and grabbed it. It was something that we were all very fortunate to witness. Even more fortunately, from Cathy's motherly point of view, he missed his prey that one time. The ducks waded into the brush and waited there until our boat left the area.

Later that night, as I lay in bed, I reflected on the similarity between the ducks and our own lives. Everything seemed to be running just the way it should. As we waded through our day-to-day existence as a family, life was just happening. Then, suddenly, death swooped down to attack us like sitting ducks. Luckily, its claws missed us this time. I wondered at this. Is this simply the natural order of life that I just somehow have to accept? The potential for death is just a part of life, isn't it? Animals live and die every day. It's how the food chain works. Were those fish we caught and threw back into the water now processing their recent brush with death? Was the family of ducks cowering under that brush still? I didn't think so. So why was I?

After falling asleep for a couple of hours, I awoke, as I had before, around 1:30 a.m., with a disturbing feeling. What was this feeling about? I didn't know. I got dressed this time, and walked into the boys' room to see if everyone was all right. All four of them were peacefully sprawled out on sleeping bags, pillows, blankets, clothing, and toys, arms and legs entwined, snoring away. They were certainly at peace. I longed for that, and for the connection they had to one another.

I walked into the kitchen, got myself a drink of water, and

gazed out the window. It was so dark and silent. Turning on the patio light, I could still only see about twelve feet into the night, then it all turned to blackness. The darkness scared me. What was out there beyond those trees? It seemed there was something waiting for me. I turned and walked into the living room, looking out through the picture window toward the lake. It was too dark to see it. Again, my eyes could only see about ten to twelve feet from the house, and the possibility of what stood beyond my sight chilled me. I checked that the doors were locked. They were, of course. I had checked them several times before I went to bed.

I knew that I wasn't going to be able to sleep. I grabbed the Tom Brown book I had been reading, *The Tracker,* and lay down on the couch in the living room. As I read, I had the strange sensation that someone was watching me. There were many windows from which to look out during the day, but at night I couldn't see anything. Anything could be looking in at me.

Just as I started to get into the reading I thought I heard a noise outside. I abruptly turned off the reading light, leapt to one of the windows, and strained my eyes to see. Nothing there, nothing that could be seen, anyway. Returning to the couch and my reading, I felt disgust. Why was I so afraid? This was one of the safest places on earth! Why did I lock the doors? What was it in that darkness beyond the trees that scared me so much? I heard a noise again. This time I turned off the light and waited by the window. If there was something out there, I was going catch it with my eyes. It wasn't going to play tricks on me anymore. Then I heard it, a muffled screeching sound. My heart jumped, but then I noticed that the wind had picked up slightly, and I was pretty sure it was a branch rubbing against the gutter right above me. That made me even madder at myself.

"You must run into the rooooooooar." I imitated Kosan's

voice and chuckled. "Yeah, Kosan, right! I'm a coward! I am such a coward!"

"No, Grant. You must run into the rooooooooar or you will not be free," I said to myself as if I were Kosan.

I can't believe what a coward I am. If they could only see me now, peering through this window into the night, locked away in my terror, paralyzed! Would they award this brave warrior the knobkerrie then? My eyes filled with righteous rage. *What the hell is my problem? There's nothing out there! There's nothing beyond those trees!*

A voice popped into my head that said, *Prove it!*

OK, I will. I will run into the roar!

I unlocked the door, threw it open, and bolted out into the night, charging into the darkness that I feared so much. "Ahhh-hhhhhhhgh!" I cried out. "Ahhhhhhhhhgh!" It was a cry of utter terror and utter determination. It was my warrior cry!

I ran down the driveway into the woods. Now surrounded by complete darkness, I stopped, huffing and puffing to catch my breath. *Nothing here! Remarkable. No ghosts! No bears! No killers roaming the night!* I smiled with warrior pride. I had faced this darkness down.

Then I heard another noise, not more than twenty feet away. My heart jumped. I looked over. "Not this time, you bastard!" I shouted and launched off again into the darkness, toward the direction of the unidentified noise in the woods. "Ahhhhhhhhhgh!" I screamed out again. I ran and ran into the shadows, dodging brush and trees as they appeared before me in the darkness. Again I stopped and panted to catch my breath. "Nothing! Nothing again!" I barked out into the night. There was nothing out here, nothing to be afraid of.

A few seconds later, I heard twigs breaking and a large branch fall in the darkness not too far from where I was standing. *Oh crap!* I said to myself. *That really is something.* Another branch broke. *I'd better go!* I turned and walked very quickly toward the dim light of the house about fifty yards away. Another twig snapped, and I broke into a run. I ran as fast as I possibly could, dodging trees, jumping over rocks and logs. *Where did all these obstacles come from?* I asked myself as I ran in terror. *They weren't here when I ran out here.* I imagined a dark monster only feet behind me, ready to lash out and hook me at any moment. But I realized as I ran that I heard nothing behind me. All was silent.

As I approached the house I began to slow down, not because I was less afraid but because I was out of gas. I jumped up on the porch and grabbed the door. Just then a light blinded my face and a terrifying scream filled the night. "Ahhhhhhhh-hgh!"

Hearing this, I also screamed, "Ahhhhhhhhhgh!" In fact, we both screamed until I realized that it was Cathy, and then we scampered into the house, slamming and locking the door behind us.

"What is it? What's out there? What happened?" she asked as she tried to catch her breath.

"Maybe a bear, I don't know." I replied. "You scared the hell out of me!"

"Me? What on earth? I heard you screaming out there. I thought you were being eaten alive!"

It took a few minutes for me to figure out all that had happened, and then it took even longer to explain it to Cathy, and to apologize for scaring her so badly. I felt even more ashamed that I hadn't realized I might scare someone as I cried out into the night. I felt badly that I had frightened her and even pushed past her into the house. We sat in the living room and talked.

"I don't know what to do, honey," I exclaimed in exasperation. "I'm just trying to get over my fears. I'm so sick of them. I felt like it was almost working for a while out there, but then I actually did hear something and had to run. I don't know. I'm desperate. I don't know what to do. I feel like I need to make peace with God or something. I need some kind of ritual or something—a way to let this stuff go, ask for his help, get back on my feet. In some ways I feel like I'm beginning to get better, but I need a push. I'm at a loss as to how to get there."

"I know. I feel it too," she responded in a gentle and reflective voice. "There's a spiritual aspect to this that I don't quite understand. It's as if we've been living out some sort of spiritual drama. We need a higher power to pull us out of this. Grant, I need you to be there. I know I don't always react to things the way you do. I was really quiet on the plane because I sort of go into this denial thing that later begins to open up. I'm dealing with it now! When I saw Steven and knew that he was all right I just relaxed, but that's changed. Now I have a hard time letting him out of my sight. He's sick, you know."

"What's wrong?" I felt a wave of fear pass through me from very deep within.

"Oh, he's got a high fever and wheezing. He's not going to be better in time to go to camp. He'll have to stay with us." The fear passed quickly at those words. Though I was concerned about his sickness, I was relieved that he would not be leaving us as planned. I realized how difficult it would have been to leave him there with other adults even if he had been completely healthy. It was just too much for me and Cathy. This sickness was the excuse we needed to keep him with us, close at our sides, just the three of us for the next six days.

"Hey, maybe that's good. I don't think either of us would get too much vacation with him out of our sight. This way we can be with him and take good care of him. We'll all be better off if he stays."

Tomorrow was the last day with all of the boys. The following day I would drive them down toward Oxford, Wisconsin, to be with their peers at camp. I wanted to do something special with them before we separated as a family. "Can you think of anything we could do to bring the family together one more time in some meaningful way before they go? Maybe we could do some sort of ritual or worship service. That might help me get beyond this fear and stuff as well."

"How about a sweat lodge?" she replied, turning to walk down the hall and back to bed.

A sweat lodge? I thought to myself. *Yes! That would be a great way to do something cleansing and spiritual at the same time. It would be a perfect way to ask God to remove my fear and give me strength, and at the same time bond the family together! Tomorrow night will be the older boys' last night with us. It would be a good experience for all of us. I could build it right down by the lake.* I was excited. As I prepared to go back to bed, I made preliminary plans. There was some wood and a few old tarps in the shed. It would be an ugly lodge, but it would do the trick. I could get some rocks over on the road to Szantay's Point and build the thing right next to the water! We could go for a midnight dip afterward! It would be perfect.

17

AFRAID OF THE DEEP

It was late evening on the last day our family would be together in this special place. Tomorrow three boys would leave for their camp. I had prepared everything for our final ceremony.

"OK, let's get down there. The rocks should be red hot by now," I barked as the family sat around the living room of our cabin reading and talking to one another. I was feeling on edge, tight, and cranky. It was ten o'clock in the evening, and my chest seemed to be turning inside out. But the notion that I'd soon be in prayer in the lodge's hot steam gave me a sense of solace. Cathy stood up from the couch, where she had been sitting quietly with Steven, who was feeling a little better. His fever had gone down to just above normal, and he was very talkative between his coughing and wheezing.

"I think I'm going to skip the lodge and stay with Steven," she informed us.

"But, Mom." Steven paused and coughed a bit.

"Can't we go and sit down on the dock next to the lodge while they're in there?"

"That's a good idea." Cathy grabbed a blanket from the couch. "But wrap yourself up in this, and you'll have to go to bed soon."

The three other boys stripped down to their shorts, grabbed a few flashlights and towels, and waited by the door. They were eager to get into the lodge. It was an exciting experience for young men: nakedness (now that Mom wasn't going to be in it), fire, rocks, earth, water, sweat—all the things a boy would ever want in one place. Add in the spiritual aspect of prayer and meditation, and some Native American ritual, and it became a mysterious and sacred experience for them.

The lodge was far from authentic. In fact, when I set out to build it that afternoon, I realized that it would be a waste to kill saplings, find twine, and do all the things I'd have to do to create a lodge anything like what the Native Americans would have built. I realized we'd only be using it a few times, and would then have to take it down before we left for home. So I built a makeshift lodge from some old fence posts and blue and green plastic tarps I found near the cabin. The lodge was a rectangular structure with a low ceiling, covered in plastic tarps and sealed all around with logs lying pressed against the tarps. It sat not more than five feet from the lake, next to a low brick fireplace where I heated the rocks. I dug a shallow pit in the center of the dirt floor for the hot rocks and placed the seat cushions from the boat around the pit for our seats. It took me all day to build it, to find stones for heating in the fire, and to build a good fire that would last a few hours in the gentle wind coming off the lake.

While I had been working on the lodge I tried to keep my mind on spiritual things, something like a holy state of prayer. I asked God to free me from my fears, to help me to understand. I prayed that this lodge would be healing, and that all of us would benefit from it. I prayed that I might truly find the missing piece of my inner being to fill that void and darkness within. I had the sense that this lodge would play a special role in the days to come, because at one point, while I was working to tie down the tarp over the structure, I heard the shriek of a large bird and looked up to see the eagle soaring well above the lake near Szantay's Point. He flew high in the sky and glided in circles in the wind. I felt that he was honoring my noble intentions for this ancient ritual, regardless of how ugly and un-Indian-like my lodge really was. The lodge having been built, the rocks collected, and the fire lit, the only remaining task was to keep an eye on the fire during and after dinner to make sure it burned hot enough to get the rocks to the right temperature.

As we all walked down the path leading to our lakeside sweat lodge, I felt a bit of inner determination come over me. I had grown impatient with feeling so bad, so fearful, so wounded. Enough was enough! I was going to beat this thing! Something was missing, and I had to find out what it was. I was resolved to figure it out during this meditative time in the lodge, and I'd stay in there until I had the answer.

The path forked in front of the water. The right branch led to the dock, where Cathy and Steven peeled off and made themselves comfortable in two beach chairs so they could sit quietly and look at stars. The path to the left brought us immediately to the lodge.

"Are the rocks hot?" Ronnie walked around the lodge to look at the fire on the other side. "Dad, the rocks don't look too hot."

I rushed over to look. The fire was burning fairly intensely, but the rocks were not red-hot, which was always best. I was disappointed. "No, they don't look too hot, but they'll have to do."

"Why don't we wait a while?" Ronnie offered a reasonable

solution, but my inner anxious state couldn't wait any longer. It was now or never.

"Nah. Let's do it now."

We grabbed two shovels and proceeded to dig the rocks out of the coals, to blow the ashes off each of them, and to place them inside the lodge. This took about five minutes. Then the four of us men plowed into the dark lodge, sealing the opening behind us.

At first we sat there in silence, accustoming ourselves to our new abode. The light from the fire right outside the lodge flickered in the wind, causing shadows of light and darkness to dance on the tarpaulin walls surrounding us. All was quiet except the occasional gentle and muffled voices of Cathy and Steven speaking to each other from the nearby dock.

I dropped a few sprinkles of tobacco on the rocks and said a few words. I had no sage or sweet grass, but pipe tobacco would do. The Native Americans used it in many of their ceremonies. I asked for divine guidance and honored God and also Mother Earth. I silently asked for the spirit of Kosan to enter the lodge with his wisdom, and for Mablevi's and Albert's courage, and for Simeon's big heart. I asked that the spirit of Lachy be with us here, and all the good grandfathers who had gone before (I didn't want the bad ones, especially my relatives). I then ceremonially honored the four directions, which represent different states of human life. The north represents the hard road, times of trial. I could certainly relate to that. The east represents enlightenment and new birth—something I needed. The south is linked to fruit and success. I wished for this for our entire family. The west represents death—a state that I feared so much, except that I recognized that something in me had to die in order for me to really live. I prayed openly not to be afraid of death and to honor the spiritual deaths that must take place in our lives. Swedenborg had said that the old person must die in order for the new to be conceived. I could see this so clearly in my own life. With the honoring of each direction I poured a bit of water on the rocks and steam hissed forth, ascending and filling the lodge with a wet warmth. Soon the warmth turned to heat. It wasn't the hottest lodge I'd ever been in, but it was hot. The boys breathed deep and gently sighed as they tried to cope with the heat, and I continued the ceremony.

As is the custom that I had learned, after the initial ceremony there was time for each person to have a chance to pray. This began with the son on my left and followed around in a circle until all of us had prayed. When each person was finished, more water was poured onto the hot rocks, and the heat of the lodge would intensify. As my sons prayed, I listened. Though their prayers were simple, they were very powerful. Each thanked the Creator for life, and for his family and friends. They prayed for their friends at home who were struggling, for the strength to do the right thing. They gave thanks for the vacation time, and for the adventure to come at the boys' club camp they'd enter tomorrow. I was blown away by their prayers, especially since I felt such cynicism inside myself. I felt anger at my decrepit emotional condition. Unlike me, they prayed with faith. Their prayers seemed like angels whispering words of love to God and to one another. Their depth of spiritual maturity filled me with pride. Perhaps I hadn't done too bad a job as a father after all. They were praying and wanting to grow and to do the right thing. These prayers never came from my lips at their age. Their confidence in God far exceeded mine.

Sitting in the stillness of the dark lodge, I began to reflect deeply on my life. I remembered that when I was a young boy I used to dream I could fly far from the loneliness I felt so acutely at home, from the darkness and gloom. As a child I searched for God out there. There were plenty of good experiences outside of home. As a boy, I walked in meadows and deep forests, drinking in the stillness next to flowing brooks. But I was alone. Even when I was with friends, I felt alone. And I kept moving, afraid of the footsteps behind me, afraid of that darkness I faced at home and the emptiness that I still faced. If I paused too long, I could hear the footsteps coming, and I would run. I ran all my life. It took different forms as I grew—fantasy, drugs, alcohol, romance, work, introversion, isolation. These were all means of running from the darkness, or the roar of the fears in my life. My boys never ran. They stood tall and firm, with confidence and trust. I could relate to their childlike innocence, these beautiful young men, but I lost the connection when I reflected on their inner trust in life, in God, in each other. I never had that.

When it was my turn to pray I asked God for faith and for trust. I asked him for the courage that I needed so much. When I was finished I poured two ladles of water onto the hot rocks, heating the lodge to its highest degree. We sat in silence and in meditation, listening to the hissing rocks, watching the dance of the firelight and praying silently within.

The sweat poured out of my body, trickling down my forehead and into my eyes, and tears rolled out to wash away the salt. I saw that my little boys were becoming men. They prayed like men, full of visions and safety and a courage I did not know. They were brothers who bonded together in every way—wandering companions in this spiritual forest we call life. I longed for that. I sat there in the heat and reflected more deeply. I thought of my own brother, and how different life would have been if he hadn't died. I wondered what my life would have been like with him, if his life were not cut short. I imagined him as a child growing as I had grown. Would he have walked the same fields I had walked, and sipped the streams I had sipped? I imagined him, just as he had been in the only photo I had ever seen of him, sitting quietly next to the waters, arms and chest bare to the world, his little body bent over the edge, gazing outward and beyond.

Holding this picture of him in my mind, I realized that our worlds would never touch. I had faith that there was, indeed, life after death. But there seemed to be a great barrier between these two worlds. Separated at that point where life and death meet, I could only imagine him. In my mind's eye I saw him again, and I looked into his face and eyes as he quietly stared off into the horizon far beyond the water's edge. His bent brow hinted of a deeper contemplation, a deep wisdom and a sadness. Perhaps it reflected a grief for someone he loved, or maybe a knowledge too sad for a little boy, an awareness of a day to come or a day gone by. I saw myself in that face, and I cried.

And then, as if my imagination took on a life of its own, he walked away through the woods until he disappeared from my sight. It was hard enough for me to imagine this, but to think of my mother and father's anguish when he left them forever for heaven. I remembered the story that had been told to me later in life, that they had dressed him in his favorite outfit as they prepared him for eternal rest—the last time they saw him in this earthly life.

Reflecting on my own life, I felt so alone. I thought of myself as a boy again, alone in the woods. I hacked my way through the thick vines of entangled thoughts and fears, and all my life I struggled up the rocky incline toward the safety of the top of the hill. The hill was accomplishment, popularity, success. And yet as that boy I kept deep within me almost a hidden fear of the unknown, the darkness and the void I didn't understand at the time. They were my personal monsters and shadows I did my best to hide from to protect my inner self. To use Kosan's metaphor, I ran from the lions that hunted me relentlessly, desiring to eat my flesh and take away my soul. Now praying to God in this lodge, I wondered how close he truly was to me. I was definitely a believer all my life, but God seemed so far away. Would he be able to be there for me now? I could only have faith, if not absolute trust—something I was still trying to cultivate within myself.

I ended our time of meditation and prayer with words of thanks. "Thank you, God, for this time, for brothers, for families, for friends. God, thank you for visions, and for the love in our hearts. Love hurts sometimes, but that's what makes us feel alive. We thank you for life." My final prayers, spoken aloud, signaled the end of our sweat lodge ceremony.

The boys piled out of the lodge. I watched them carefully, curious to see what they would do next. One of the lessons I had told them was that after the ceremony you should be quiet for a while and just listen. Be still in nature. As I crawled out behind them, the light of the fire in front of me flooded my eyes, and the steam of the lodge poured out of the opening, creating a fog all around. I paused and waited for my eyes to adjust. I looked up at the stars. They were magnificent. The Milky Way lit up the sky above. The lake was quiet and peaceful, and this time the stillness brought me peace rather than anxiety. I felt peace! I felt whole, if only for a moment. Ronnie, Jason, and Owen stood in silence at the foot of the water and stared into the sky. They did not speak. I smiled that they had learned so quickly and were now enjoying the oneness they most certainly felt with the world.

As soon as I stopped and stood beside them they looked at each other, and without a spoken word, simultaneously headed into the water. The three of them walked into the lake until they were neck-deep in the dark waters, and they treaded water there together in the silence of the night.

I heard Steven whisper to his mother on the dock, "Look Mom, they're going into the water." The two of them were still nestled in blankets out on the dock, staring at the stars.

"Dad!" Jason called to me. "Come out here. It's really something. Just walk straight into the water until you are over your head. It's something else."

I took a few steps forward into the water but stopped as it reached my knees. It was cold, and I was one of those people who liked warm water. Besides, it was night, and I was a little concerned that none of us should be out swimming over our heads after a steam bath like that sweat lodge we just experienced. Somebody could faint and drown.

"Come on, Dad!" Jason's voice rang out over the waters.

"No, I don't think so. I think you guys should come in. It's too dangerous to be out there."

"No, Dad. Come on!" Ronnie tried this time.

"No. Come in!" I could feel a growing lump in my throat and the fear that something bad was going to happen. They didn't answer me. I could hear them talking to one another in a gentle and friendly tone. There were a few giggles as they continued to swim in the darkness, about thirty feet out from the dock.

"Come in, Dad!" Jason tried again.

"No! You come in." They ignored me.

Standing knee-deep on the edge of the water, I could feel that a part of me wanted to go, but something stronger held me back. Why wouldn't I go? I could be out there with my sons! I just couldn't do it. The fears were stopping me once again. I felt shame that I, their father and brother, wouldn't join them out there. I tried to cast off the shame by telling myself, *At least they have each other.*

As I stood on the edge of the water, I felt like I was standing on the edge of their dreams. Because they had no fear, they could go wherever they desired and do whatever they felt called to do. I couldn't do that. And because I couldn't do that, I had too many days of solitude. Brotherless, I stood alone too many times. My only brother was shut away deep within my mother's dresser drawer, behind too many doors that I had locked for fear of the darkness. Too many days of my life were spent in a foggy daze of alcoholic escapades. Too many times I swallowed hard to keep down the pain and the memory of something, perhaps someone I didn't even know. Too many times I stopped short on the shoreline, afraid to go the distance, afraid to trust, to live, to leave the loneliness. What was I afraid of? What was I running from? Was it death? It most certainly was! But it was not my death that I ran from. It was the death of my brother!

It was the death of my brother that haunted me. I shivered at that realization. I thought hard about it on that lonely shoreline. It seemed to be true. Too many times I heard those footsteps following behind, and I ran from my brother and all the mystery and fear surrounding him. I could hear those unspoken words I heard so many times before: *It's a dangerous, dangerous world. Anything can happen. Anyone can be taken any time. If you get sick, you will die, because, because . . .* The voice inside never finished that sentence, instead leaving a void as big as this lake in my soul. I finished the sentence there on the beach. *Because Bruce died!* I was running from my brother and all the darkness associated with him. I was running from my brother, who left me before I was born.

18

GUIDEPOSTS AND
GUARDIANS

The ride down to the boys' club camp with my three
elder sons went by quickly. We talked about the
lodge the night before, and they pleasantly chided
me for not following them into the water. I confessed to them that I was afraid, and assured them
that it really was dangerous to swim in the dark
after a sweat lodge. They laughed at my warning,
brushing it off as another one of Dad's unwarranted
concerns. However, I also sensed in their laughter
that they understood my state of mind and that
they forgave me for not being able to join them.

I planned to spend the night with the boys at
the camp and return the next morning. When we
arrived there, the boys at camp came to greet us
and were glad to see my sons again. The feelings
were mutual. I sat and talked with the counselors,
and we swam in the nearby lake, ate a good dinner, and turned in for the night. I don't know if it
was the change of scenery or the companionship of

lots of children and men, but I slept more soundly than I had in weeks. I awoke early in the morning refreshed and relaxed, ready for the trip back to the Northwoods.

Soon others woke up, and breakfast was served to the boys. I began to pack my things for the trip home. Randy Rhodes, the head counselor, stopped me and asked if I would be willing to give the boys a little talk before I left. It wasn't too often that they had a minister up there, and they thought it might be a nice way to start the boys' day. I said that I would be happy to. I didn't know what I would say, but I had about five minutes to think about it.

As the boys gathered around me in a semicircle outside the cabin, I thought I'd talk to them about fear and courage. They were on my mind. I decided to tell them a couple of stories. I started by telling them about our crazy plane ride to and from JFK airport. I didn't overdo it, but I spoke of my fear and not knowing what would happen next. I then told them of my adventure traveling into the townships of Claremont and Soweto in South Africa, and how I prayed for courage, and how funny it was that these truly brave men who lived there, and who dealt with so many terrible things, honored me with a gift for a warrior. I then told them how I had met a true war hero who fought in Vietnam and saved people's lives, and how another one did the same thing, but he died doing it, and that there was no greater love than to lay down one's life for his friends.

All this time I was speaking, I really didn't know what my point was, or whether I wasn't telling these stories for me to hear rather than for the gathering of boys to hear, but they listened intently. The point, it turned out, was that life is real. It takes its turns, and sometimes it can get scary, but you've got to move on. Sometimes you're called upon to do things you wouldn't normally do if you didn't have to. It's at those times it helps to call upon the Lord, to ask for his help, and to just do the best you can. That's all Lachy was trying to do, and Jeremy's brother Rick. That's all the brave people in South Africa were trying to do, to live, to do the right thing, to do the best they could—and somehow they rose above their fears.

As I spoke, I recognized that this was all I was trying to do for myself. I realized that even though I felt fear, I continued on my journey and performed the duties before me. I got back on that same plane and flew across the world. I journeyed into the heart of Soweto. I stayed there. I gave them my all, even though the news of my boy left me with little energy to give. Hearing myself speak, I realized that I had been carrying a great deal of shame about my fears, and that I didn't have to. I had every right to be afraid. I had every right to be shaken. More than this, I had not stopped short of my mission there, or in any tasks that subsequently fell before me. This gave me solace. As I finished my talk, the boys spontaneously clapped and cheered. I smiled and waved like some rock star finishing his encore. Though their brief cheer was one for all the heroes, and for a new day at camp, the sound of their voices lifted me into a sense of new pride of inner accomplishment and realization. I heard it as the cheer of victory. I realized I was beginning to feel a lot better. I was healing.

Just before leaving, I gathered my three sons and gave them my usual lecture. "Don't swim alone. Don't go behind the shooting range when people are shooting. Don't do anything stupid. Don't eat anything you don't recognize. Stay out of trouble. And have a good time." They groaned and nodded in compliance, giving me the usual assurances, and I left them there in the clearing near the cabin as I drove off in my car. I must confess that as I watched them disappear in my rearview mirror, I prayed for their well-being, and that angels would watch over them. It was hard to leave them.

I made good time driving back to Hazelhurst and the

Northwoods. Cathy met me at the driveway. It was touching to see her sense of relief at my return. I told her that I was beginning to feel a lot better. It was as if a weight was lifting off of me. We talked as I unpacked and readied supper for the three of us. Cathy said that Steven was doing much better, with only a cough and a runny nose but no fever. It was good to be back in the quiet of the Northwoods with Cathy and Steven.

The next two days were spent somewhat the same as the days before, but with fewer people. We slept in, went fishing and swimming, read books, went shopping, and explored different parts of the woods. We had a very quiet and peaceful time together. It was good to spend so much time with not only Cathy, but with Steven. He had our full attention, and we talked about so many things. It was our time to cherish him and to show him how much we loved him and appreciated his presence. Together, Steven and I cleared a special place under a tree near the lake to sit and to just be with nature. I called it "our safe and sacred place," and it was magical for both of us. Underneath a large, old cedar tree, with moss growing on the ground and flowers and other pretty branches of trees and leaves placed all around, we sat in our quiet cove and just listened, only talking occasionally.

Cathy also spent special time with Steven. She created a treasure hunt with maps hidden all over the woods and parts of the lake. She followed Steven as he left on his adventure to find the various maps leading to treasure. One map took him to Szantay's Point, which Cathy had named "the home of Gendor, the dragon prince." Another map took him to "the Cove of Peace and Enchantment," where he'd find another map. In the end, he came to a treasure buried under some leaves near our cabin. It contained candles, beads, and feathers from a Native American store in town, books, and some small toys. Steven was delighted.

It was the fourth night alone with Steven and Cathy that I reflected once again on my emotional predicament—this time with a serious breakthrough. I was just about finished reading Tom Brown's book *The Tracker* when I came across an intriguing little story. Tom grew up near the Pine Barrens of New Jersey, and the book is about his adventures there. He described how one night he was sleeping alone in the middle of the Pine Barrens, and he heard something in the woods near him. He thought immediately that it must be the Jersey Devil, which is New Jersey's version of Bigfoot—with a bite. He talked about how this darkness seemed to hover nearby and how he shook in fear. But then, as if some unseen force grew within him, he jumped up and chased the thing through the woods. The next day, as morning broke, he looked for tracks, and there were only his. He wondered at this and came to the conclusion that the Jersey Devil was probably nothing more than a reflection of the darkness inside of him.

That idea struck me. Not less than a week ago I was running into that same darkness, trying to chase away my monsters. I was intrigued by the idea that it was not something out there that I feared, but something inside me. It made so much sense—the darkness I had feared was the darkness in me. The darkness I had run from was the void in my life. Again I thought of Bruce. He seemed to be the answer. He was a mystery to me growing up, the unseen reason for all that fear in my mother all those years, the unseen reason for the unspoken grief of both my parents, the deafening quietness, the emptiness that silently cried out to be filled.

My sister Beth Ann had confessed to me that they were never able to talk about Bruce's death. She spoke of her loneliness and confusion. The whole family remained in silence and in darkness about it all the days of our lives together. Some people talk about the elephant in the living room that no one will acknowledge. In our case, it was the silence, the pain, the muffled screams of grief that turned into a monster that haunted us. That void, that quiet darkness, that rumbling tumult that groaned, stirred, and silently cried out just beyond our consciousness was enough to scare any child, and any adult child as well. I gasped as I realized that, contrary to what I had assumed previously, it wasn't Bruce that I was running from. It was the lack of him. This realization gave me pause. It seemed very significant. Something in my stomach moved as the knowledge came to me; the fears moved, as if they were briefly bumped aside for a moment.

I sat quietly by myself for some time as Cathy and Steven headed off to bed. I knew something was brewing inside me. I was waking up to some insight that I hadn't seen before. I went over some of my realizations again and again, trying to see what was still missing. My thoughts fired off in random and rapid succession. I was afraid because I had been shaken. I was afraid because I had a childhood full of fear. I felt so alone, even though I had friends. I didn't have to lock doors. I didn't have to stop on the shoreline. I could keep going, regain courage. I had lived through the brushes with death, and Steven had lived. I thought of Lachy and what he told me. He had lived. Yes, Rick had died. But sometimes that happens. Lachy had lived, Rick had died. I had lived, Bruce had died. But why so much fear? Again I thought of Lachy's story, and longed for a hand to reach down and pull me out of this desolate state I was in. Again, something moved inside.

I longed for Lachy's sense of peace, and his bravery. What a good big brother he'd make. I needed to talk to him. He could give me that hand I needed. But I couldn't call him. I didn't know his phone number, and it was too late to call, close to 1 a.m. on the East Coast. So many thoughts went through my mind, and I mulled over these points again and again, seeing if the fears would budge, seeing if an answer would surface. As I sat there alone, I longed even more to talk to someone. But it was really too late to call anyone. I stared at the clock on the wall.

Who can I call?

A voice like a whisper inside my head answered me. *Call him. He's there for you.*

I thought about it. *Lachy's a nice guy. Heck! He's a real soldier, and he'd understand if I called this late. I can get his number from information.* Moments later I was on the phone with Lachy Brown.

"Lachy Brown."

"Lachy? This is Grant. I'm so sorry to call you at this hour."

"Grant? No problem, buddy." He paused for a moment to gain his senses. I knew I had awakened him. "Dorothy and I had a late night with the kids. I just got in bed a half hour ago. Couldn't really sleep anyway. What's up? Are the fears coming on strong? Battling your demons?"

"Well, I have been. This place is dark at night. They're out there in the darkness, just beyond the shadows. I just wanted to talk for a minute, maybe get a little big brotherly advice."

"I'd be happy to help. Is it the fear of death that's got you?"

"No, actually, I think I might be getting better about that."

"Yeah? That's great!"

"Well, I'm not cured but it seems to not have hold of me the way it did. And I think it's related to a few insights. Remember we talked about my brother Bruce? And how all this fear might be related to his death? I'm thinking that this darkness has to do with him. Not just the darkness, but I think I've been running from the pain, the fear, the emptiness surrounding his death. Nothing was ever said, but it had to be there. Maybe because it was never spoken of, it became something to be feared and to escape from."

"Whoa. Even hearing that gives me a shiver. Something tells

me you're on to something. I mean it. I had this strange shiver come over me. Hah. Maybe I'm just waking up."

"I felt pretty alone growing up. I look at my own boys and the love they share. I wish I had a brother to be there for me, to show me the way."

"Well, maybe you did. You believe in guardian angels, don't you? Maybe Bruce has that job. Maybe he's been looking after you. Why not? He's got to be the most kindred spirit you have on the other side."

My heart jumped and began to burn. I had heard this suggestion before but simply could not believe it. Why couldn't I believe this? How much I wished this were true. But it couldn't be. "Bruce is just a little celestial baby. I'm all by myself."

Lachy didn't accept this answer. "Grant, you're not his big brother. He's *your* big brother. He's not a kid anymore. He's grown. He's a grown man in heaven, an angel. Hey, you're the minister here! You know the score! He's an angel! He's your big brother! Something inside tells me I'm right. He's definitely with you. Man, I'm shivering all over."

"Me too. Wow! I suppose anything is possible. And I have thought about him being around, I suppose, but not as my older brother. What a revelation.... I don't know. I'm not sure I can buy it. I appreciate the thought but maybe this is just wishful thinking."

"Yeah," Lachy interjected sarcastically. "OK. Big warrior man. You're all alone, and you've been fighting these battles all by yourself. You're the only one in this universe, the only one who fights alone without any help from heaven. You think you can beat these demons all by yourself? Man, good luck! Where's your faith?"

"Guardian angels, huh?"

"Well, some of these angels no doubt become our guardians, right?"

"Yeah."

"Well? I know I believe in them. I wouldn't be here without them. They were there to pick me up when I needed them."

"All right. It gives me something to think about. I appreciate you taking some time with me." We talked for another ten minutes about more trivial things. It was a way for both of us to sort of calm down. There was something about this conversation that had us both shivering. It was something to really ponder, and I had to allow it to sink in. After thirty or so years of thinking I was, indeed, alone, it would take time to have that sense begin to shift. As we said goodbye I apologized again for calling him so late. He told me that he was glad I called. He had been thinking about me a lot and appreciated the connection. He urged me to call any time. I hung up the phone and began to prepare for bed.

I turned off the lights in the living room and headed off to the bathroom to brush my teeth. As I turned on the water and looked in the mirror I thought to myself, *Wow. I wish I could believe what Lachy said. So. Um. Bruce, are you with me?* I shivered a bit at the thought. I listened. I looked around. *Well, maybe you're asleep. Time for bed.* I brushed my teeth, put the toothbrush back into its holder, and shut off the faucet. I turned to go back into the kitchen to check that the doors were locked. I stopped halfway down the hallway. *Nope. Not tonight. Tonight, the doors stay unlocked. This is a safe place. We'll be protected.* I turned the other way, walked down the hall, entered our bedroom, and quietly climbed into bed. I soon fell asleep.

19

MY BIG BROTHER!

That night, as Cathy and I slept with Steven sick in bed beside us, coughing and wheezing the night away, I awoke from a most amazing dream. It was more meaningful and real than any dream I had before. It was a dream that would change my life forever.

I dreamed I was a little boy, walking in the forests I used to know so well as a child. It was springtime, and the light green leaves whispered to each other as a warm breeze gently moved them. I walked a familiar path through a shallow swamp with the scent of skunk cabbage and wet earth in my nostrils. A few small birds flew in and out of the brush on either side of me. I was barefoot, bare-chested, and wearing just a pair of white shorts. But I felt quite warm and peaceful.

I came to a familiar clearing where a large oak tree hung over a bend in the stream. It was a place I would often go as a child to fish for minnows and hunt for crayfish. I looked up into the tree and could see the sun shining through its branches and leaves, creating a dazzling display of light and shadow on the ground below. The shadow and light seemed to dance together in harmony upon the earth and the water, where tiny sparkles of light would appear and disappear like fairies playing hide and seek.

The tree's partially exposed roots extended a foot or two out over the water. I sat down on them and looked down into the deeper part of the stream just below me. I stared quietly and waited, searching the water with my eyes. I don't know what I was searching for, whether it was minnows, crayfish, frogs, or something much greater and more meaningful. My brow furrowed in deep concentration. I felt a sadness inside, and a loneliness, and a longing, but for what I did not know.

As I continued to search, I heard rustling of leaves on the path behind me, the path I had just taken. I turned and heard a strong but gentle voice speak. A man's voice. He said, "Little brother!"

I looked up and saw a man coming toward me. He smiled with love and a deep warmth. As I got a better view of his face, I laughed a little, because he looked a lot like me. But he was older, stronger, and I could see in his eyes that he was wiser. The kindness in his manner confirmed to me that he was my brother. As he crouched down to look into my face, he extended his hand toward me, and then, lifting it, he touched my face. As I felt his hand rest on my temple and cheek, I burst into tears, knowing he had found me. For the first time in all my days of solitude, I saw, felt, knew my brother—my *big* brother. Within a moment, in a touch, in a child's cry, I awoke.

Sitting up in bed, the twilight of early morning filling the lake, trees, and cabin with a dim and subtle light, I opened my eyes wide to see. With Cathy sleeping soundly beside me on my left, and Steven asleep in a cot on my right, I spoke out loud as if it were midday and they were at the kitchen table beside me.

"I have a brother!" The words bounced around our bedroom and broke the silence. "I have a brother!"

"What?" Cathy asked in sort of a confused moan. She rolled over to face me and tried to open her eyes to see what I was up to.

"I have a big brother!" I felt the wetness in my eyes begin to roll down my cheeks.

"What do you mean?" she asked. "Oh, you had a dream. Can you tell me about it later?"

I realized that she wasn't going to understand what this dream meant to me, at least not at six in the morning. So I told her to go back to sleep, and I got up and ran into the bathroom to share the good news with the reflection in the mirror.

I cried as I told that image of myself, again and again, "I have a brother! I have a big brother!" As tears poured out of my eyes, mucous flowed from my nose. I cried like a two-year-old, like I hadn't in thirty-six years! It was not so much the intellectual realization that a brother had come before me. It was a deep, heartfelt, gut-level sensation, felt for the first time, that I had a real older brother. I was not the only son. I was a second son, the little son. I wasn't number one. I was number two! And though words cannot adequately describe what that meant to my inner being, it filled me with relief. It filled me with humility, with wonder, with a sense of inner peace that I had never felt before. It blew the fears right out of my chest and onto the floor. For that brief moment the emptiness in my heart, the void inside of me, was filled.

What happened next was so real and seemed so natural that I do not doubt it. Somewhere between a mental process and a vision, the darkness that I feared for so long came into the bathroom with me. This darkness turned to light and became a human being. Taking the form of the man in my dream, he sat right beside me. He spoke to me silently, as if through some sort of transfer of thoughts and emotions, all in a single moment. "Finally you let me grow up." With those words came a tremendous sigh of relief and release of sadness. "I have always been your big brother. I have always been there. And I always will be." Then, as quickly as he had come, he was gone again. I stood in the bathroom alone once more.

I felt no fear. The whole occurrence seemed natural. I didn't even know whether Bruce had really come to talk to me, or whether somehow a mental process inside of me took outward form. It didn't really matter. I knew and felt for the first time that I actually had a real big brother, and this was a relief to me. I knew he was alive in heaven, and that he was as human and full of feeling as I was. I knew he was with me, just on the other side of that thin veil that separates life and death. Our lives were as close as the shadow and light that danced together in my dream.

I walked into the living room and sat down, thinking over what had just happened. The more I thought about it, the more remarkable it seemed. I may have been wishing to see my brother, and perhaps the dream of him could have been created by my wishful thinking. But his visit to the bathroom was unsolicited. I was puzzled that he first came as the darkness, but upon further reflection realized that this is how I had been viewing him for so long—in fact, all my life. He came as the darkness and then took on a bright human form because I was ready to see him for what he really was. I had come to that realization on my own, that he was behind the darkness I ran away from, and now he could emerge as the real brother he had always been. He was finally able to take a human form in my conscious mind.

His words, and the manner in which he spoke them, had been a surprise to me. *"Finally you have let me grow up!"* I never would have imagined these to be his first words to me. I had no idea I had any effect on him at all! But the emotion I felt from him as he said that, such release, such relief! How could I doubt? This wasn't my projection. This wasn't my issue. It was his, and he was finding healing even as he was giving it to me. In his release I felt release. In his relief I was discovering my own. I remembered what Kosan had said to me back in South Africa, that perhaps we are the ones who do the real haunting in the spirit world, that perhaps we hold them back. Had I been holding Bruce back from growing up? Or was Bruce relieved because I was finally getting better and growing up myself? Or were both statements true? I suppose it didn't matter. How could my life ever be the same again? I found my brother. No. My brother found me!

Cathy woke up around 8:30 a.m. and stretched on the bed. I handed her a glass of orange juice and launched into my story.

"Cathy. I had the most amazing dream," I told her.

"Yeah? Did you try to wake me up and tell me about it? I'm sorry. I was so tired."

"That's OK. I dreamed that I was a little child and that my brother, Bruce, came to me. He was older than me. It seemed so real."

"Wow!"

"When I woke up, I realized that I had a big brother. I know that sounds stupid, because I already intellectually knew that, but it was something I really hadn't felt before. He seemed so human and real. I think this is going to make a big difference to me because, you know, I was sort of mixing up Bruce and Steven—"

"Yeah. I know."

"That caused me a lot of fear. I think it's because I always thought of Bruce as some vulnerable little kid, and saw Steven the same way. Now I can see that they are different. If Bruce were alive today, he'd be in his forties. I mean, now I can feel that they are different people. But that's not the end of the story. I also got up and went into the bathroom crying about the whole thing, and then something really strange happened."

Cathy rolled out of bed and began to straighten out the sheets. I could sense that this was becoming a little too much for her, first thing in the morning. But I had to continue.

"I was in the bathroom, thinking this all over and crying and then this darkness came into the room. Now, I'm not saying this was a vision. It was almost more like a mental process. But it was real. Bruce came to me."

"You're kidding!"

"He said, 'Finally you have let me grow up.'" I started to choke up, because I could once again feel the relief and release of sadness as he said those words. "Then he said he had always been with me and always will be. He said this all in a flash, as if there were no time, or words spoken. He seemed sad at first, as if he'd suffered being held down in my heart and mind for years. But it seemed like he was totally relieved at my realization that he was my big brother, and he promised me he was there."

"Grant. That's really great. I'm glad you're going through all this. But maybe you're thinking about this too much. I don't mean that it didn't happen, but you've got to slow down a little. I don't know how much more intensity I can take." Cathy put up with a lot living with me, and she could only take so much of my emotional processes at one time. I knew that, but I had to say one more thing.

"OK. This is the last thing. His sadness and relief were a surprise to me. I had no idea he would be sad, or that somehow I might have been holding him down. But I guess I was holding him down from growing up in my own mind." I paused. "I don't know. Anyway. It was a life-changing experience. Something's in my heart now that wasn't there before. I have a big brother!"

"All right. I've got to go get some breakfast," Cathy announced as she left the room. I wondered at this. This entire experience seemed so incredibly meaningful to me, and I was sad that she didn't want to hear more. But then I thought of her father and her loneliness. Of course it was hard for her to hear about this. Here I was, finding the brother I never knew, a brother who died before I was even born, and somewhere inside of her, a little girl still cried for her father. That made me sad, and I felt sympathy. This must be too much for her. I promised myself that I wouldn't continue to talk about this throughout the day, even though I was so excited that I wanted to. But I smiled a lot that day, and looked into the sky with cheerfulness and gratitude. I had a wonderful day, paying special attention to Cathy's needs, not worrying about my own for that moment. Steven also seemed especially peaceful. Later that day, Cathy loosened up and apologized for being so abrupt with me. We had a good talk, and shared our hopes that things would be getting better now for the both of us. I knew it was a new beginning for me.

That night, the last night in the Northwoods before packing up, picking up the three boys, and heading for home, I decided to do one more sweat lodge alone. Cathy and Steven sat on the dock as they had before and watched the stars. The rocks for this lodge were the hottest ever. I had collected them from Szantay's Point, and they were very round. After I brought them into the lodge with the shovel and closed the door behind me, I stared at them as they glowed in the dark. They looked like little earths. I remembered that the Native Americans called these rocks their "elders" or "grandfathers," believing they contained wise knowledge. As the water was poured onto the rocks, this knowledge was said to be released. The rocks would speak. As I poured water onto the rocks and steam spit forth into this makeshift womb, I prayed for understanding, courage, and strength.

The rocks seemed to want to speak a strong message this night, a message of new resolve and new dreams. The steam from the rocks filled the lodge with such heat that I had to lie down on the ground to endure it. I felt the healing coolness and support of Mother Earth. I thanked her for her stability and her support. I thanked our Creator for this time in the Northwoods, and for our time together as a family, and our special time with Steven. I thanked him for the revelations about Bruce. I thanked him for the healing that I truly felt had begun. Reflecting back on the last few weeks, I realized that much of the terror I felt before had turned to mild apprehension, then to occasional worry, and now to only bouts of anxiety. I was getting better.

I realized that these weeks had been an incredible spiritual journey for me. I learned so much about pain and fear, but also about this precious life, about love, and about spirituality. If it had not been for those brushes with death, and the pain and struggle for understanding that followed, I would not have discovered the true reality of my big brother. This discovery changed my outlook on life and on death forever. I knew that I had never been alone all those years of running. I knew he had been there helping me, fighting alongside me in every one of my spiritual battles. He was the one. He was the one whom I sensed wanted to meet me as Dottie opened me up to spiritual realities. He wanted me to know that he was real, and that he was always there to help me. But I had to allow him to come to me. I had to unlock the door and let him in. I still had many questions, but I felt they would be answered in time. It didn't all make sense, but what ever does? It made enough sense. In my prayers in that lodge I resolved to learn from these experiences, and to continue my quest for trust, for bravery, and for understanding—to fulfill my personal mission to help bring more love and integrity into the world. I prayed for release of the fears that had crippled me for so long, and for new courage.

I left the lodge and went straight for the lake, swimming far and deep this time, as Steven and his mother sat on the dock and watched.

"Look, Mom," Steven whispered to his mother on the dock. "He's going where my brothers went."

I came back to the shoreline renewed, the fear seemingly washed off of me in those waters, and I knew that I was not alone anymore. I could sense my brother was with me. Perhaps as he always had been.

20

SIGNS

The next morning I woke up early, wanting to take in a few more tranquil hours in this beautiful place before packing to go home. I ate breakfast and decided to walk down to the dock to contemplate the wonderful experience I had with my brother the day before. It was a cloudy day, with a brisk, cool wind blowing from the north. I sat on the dock, gazing out over the lake, and wondered if this new realization of my big brother would help me get over my fears for good. The fears had certainly diminished since our encounter. I knew that part of this was because I had been touched by the otherworld, and that it was real. Life continues on. Death is only a transition from one life into the other. I wasn't ready for me, Steven, or anyone else in my family to make that transition, but I now felt in my heart what I had always believed in my mind—we live on after death. My encounter with my brother taught me that the separation of loved ones exists only in the thin veil between consciousness and unconsciousness, and maybe not even in that at all times. My brother had touched me, had talked to me, had shown his frailty, humanity, and passion. Because of this, I felt hope that God was even closer than I had imagined. For so many years they both seemed so far away, but perhaps they were with me all the time, not just in thought or in love, but in actual presence, one I could reach out and touch.

These thoughts also gave me hope for healing. Some of that determination and zeal to get better I had felt in the sweat lodge the night before returned. If I could continue to feel the presence of my brother, and get more in touch with the presence of God, I would be whole again, free from fear, able to fly, able to live without the dread of darkness. I wanted that so much. In fact, I decided to ask for these things right there on the dock. There is that old expression, "Be careful what you ask for, you just might get it." Well, it's true. I decided I wanted a little more of that sense of my brother's presence, and perhaps we could throw God into the equation too. I decided I would call on my brother down there on the dock. I would ask for his help and a sign of his presence. Maybe he would come back again. I looked out over the water, and into the gray sky, and I spoke out loud.

"Bruce, if you're with me, I need your help." I thought of God at the same time. "Bruce, I need you, man. I need you like never before. All these fears, I can't take them anymore. I need to know that it's a safe world, or at least that I don't have to fear and worry. I need to feel your presence. Are you with me? God, are you with me? Are any of you with me? I need you so much!" I listened for a moment. I wanted a sign from Bruce, or from God, that I wasn't alone, and that there was somebody watching over us in this whole mad affair called life. I continued to talk aloud. "Bruce, I'm not kidding. I'm calling on you like I've never called on anyone before. I need to know, brother. I need to know! Give me a sign!" I stopped, listened, and watched.

As I finished those words, a very tiny hole broke in the

clouds above the lake, and just a bit of sun broke through, still filtered by the moisture above, but enough to allow one very small beam of light to descend down onto the water. From that beam came a very light downdraft of wind, which moved a small circle of water about twenty feet out from the dock. It was about ten feet in diameter, and the water glistened within. As a west wind picked up slightly, the circle of glistening water moved toward me and grew in size. It gently spread out as it approached, and in moments encircled the dock around me. It was very beautiful. I was impressed. Certainly this symbolized the ray of hope that always exists, even on our darkest cloudy days, and that surrounds us with love and light. But that seemed sort of a drab lesson. Nothing really new about it! I wasn't satisfied.

"Not good enough!" I shouted over the water. "I want something big. I need to know you are there! Show me a sign!"

As I finished those words, I heard the ripple of a flag above my head to the left. It sounded like the flap of an eagle's wing. I looked up to my left to see the Swedish flag that hung at the top of a flagpole at the end of the dock where I was sitting. A strong breeze had moved it. However, as soon as I looked up, the sun burst through the clouds in all its fullness, directly above me and into my face, and a strong wind struck my face, and lifted the hair on my head before it became calm. The gray of the day turned to full color with the light. The sun's brilliance shined down on all of creation. I thought to myself, *Yes, God is here in all his glory. He comes when we call, and can fill our lives with light. I believe it, but there's got to be more.*

"Not good enough!" I shouted, though I could see that this event was truly a representation of God's glory. "I mean it, Bruce. I want a sign I'll never forget. I want you to come here and kick me off the dock or something. This is the last time. Please, show me you're here. Help me with my fears. I'll count to three. One! Two! Three!"

"Hi, Dad." Steven touched my shoulder from behind.

I jumped in my seat. How had he gotten down to the dock without me seeing him? Why had he shown up on the count of three? My son Steven, for whom I feared, my son who was hit by a bus and thrown forty-eight feet, my son whom I couldn't separate from my dead brother, showed up as the sign.

My first reaction was one of horror. *My God!* I thought to myself. *Is this your answer to me? I was just getting it straight that Steven was not Bruce, and that I didn't have to worry, and you give me this? Why?* I shivered as a chill passed through my body. The reality of my condition, all the fear and confusion, smashed me in the face. I became as confused as ever. Why would Steven show up as the third sign? It was wrong! It was awful! It didn't fit with what I had learned the night before. I gathered myself in Steven's presence. I put on the best face I could, still shivering from the sign.

"Hi, buddy. How are you today?"

"Oh. I'm fine. I'm feeling much better. Mom says we need to pack up to leave. Are we going to go fishing? Because if we're going to go fishing, then I'd rather do that." He hung on to the flagpole, and bounced around.

"I don't think we're going to go fishing today," I replied, still trying to sort out what had just happened.

"OK. I'll go help Mom." Content with my answer, he turned and trotted up the path to the cabin. I followed behind.

I knew that I had promised myself not to say too much to Cathy about these events that were now taking place, but this one shook me in a bad way. I had to talk to her about it. I ran up the hill to the cabin, and found her sitting on the couch in the living room. Steven was standing beside the couch in conversation with her.

"Cathy, I need to talk to you for a minute. It's really important."

I suppose she could see that I was shaken. She asked Steven

to go into his room and start packing. He cheerfully complied.

"Cathy, I have to tell you one more thing, and then I'll stop talking about all of this. But it shook me." I explained what had just happened. "I just don't get it. I had just gotten Steven and Bruce separated in my mind. But it scared me. I can't get it out of my mind that something's going to happen to Steven. What else could it mean?"

"Grant, Grant. I know why you're feeling that way, but it doesn't have to mean that. Look, I wasn't going to tell you, because I don't want you to try to make Steven something he may not want to be. We have to leave him in freedom as he grows up. But there might be another explanation. Listen, you were saying that Terry and you became ministers because of Bruce. You said that Terry always said that Bruce was around you guys. Just yesterday Steven came up to me and started talking about the Lord. He's always been such a spiritual kid, Grant."

"I know, I know. That's what makes me think he's going to be taken."

"Listen. He was talking about how much he loved to talk about the Lord, and then he smiled a very big smile, and he said he wanted to be a minister when he grew up."

"Yeah? Well, that's nice," I replied as I gained more composure. "I remember when Ronnie wanted to be a minister, and a fireman, and a lawyer all at the same time. I think every kid with a religious upbringing thinks about that at one time or another. I think it would be great if he became a minister, but I don't see how that fits with what just happened."

"What I'm saying is that maybe that sign down there was Bruce saying that he's with Steven like he's with you. Steven's always been a special boy, so sweet and open. If he becomes a minister, why wouldn't Bruce be with him too? It sounds far-fetched, but it is an explanation. It doesn't have to mean that Steven is Bruce, or that Steven is going to die or anything."

I thought about these words, and they did offer another explanation. It was something to ponder. After all, the experience the night before was so positive and reassuring. There must have been another explanation for this latest event.

"Maybe that is it," I replied. "I don't know. Well, it gives me something to think about, an alternative explanation." I thought for a few moments. Then it hit me. Perhaps, in reality, the message I received was exactly what I was looking for. Maybe I was, in fact, interpreting it wrong. How much stronger could Bruce's message be that he was with me and my family? "You're right, Cathy. Remember the doctor's words when Steven was in the hospital? He said, 'It's a miracle the boy is alive. There must have been an angel with him.' Here I was on the dock asking, 'God, Bruce, whoever, where are you in my life? Where are you when I need you?' And the answer back was, 'What do you want? I stopped your 747 from crashing, and Steven was hit by a bus, thrown forty-eight feet with barely a scratch. I'm right here. I'm right here!' Gee, I'm such an idiot. What more proof could I ever want?" The more I thought about it, the more it seemed that my call for help out on that dock was, indeed, answered, and that the answer was a strong message of love and support.

Later that morning I walked down by the lake again, this time to take down the makeshift sweat lodge. Thinking about the time together with my sons in that place, and for the revelations about Bruce, I had to smile. This contraption called a "sweat lodge" and its accompanying ceremony seemed like such an incredible gift to me. In my thanks I tried my best to return the location back to its original condition before the lodge was set there. I thought to myself that this would be not only the right thing to do, but the way the Native Americans would do it. It would be my way of saying, "I know what this land means to you, to all of us, and I care."

I disassembled the sweat lodge piece by piece, trying to do

it the same attitude with which I had built it—spiritually, with thanks, reflecting on its usefulness and the lessons learned within in it. I removed the tarps, placed the logs back in a pile near the cabin, and filled in the hole where the rocks had turned water into spitting steam. As I finished raking the ground and setting all in place as it originally was, I heard another cry of an eagle out over the water. I looked over toward Szantay's Point, and there, high above the peninsula, two eagles soared together, circling one another, catching the wind, floating upward and then down again and around. It was a beautiful image of friendship, companionship, and play. After only a moment of watching their dance in the air, one eagle peeled off and headed directly toward me. He crossed the lake and slowly descended to about tree level. With his wings spread wide, he soared directly over my head and gave another call. As that happened, I instinctively felt it to be a message. There was no doubt in my mind, because I felt it in my heart. He was saying, "Thank you."

I responded, "Yes. And thank you."

The last notable occurrence before leaving for home was simply learning another piece of local history about Hazelhurst. Just before we left, I headed over to the neighbor's house to see if any of the kids' shoes had found their way over there. The neighbor had a golden retriever who loved shoes and collected them from all the other neighbors' docks every time he roamed free. As I was there, I spoke with the man about how much we loved this place and how, even though we now lived in Pennsylvania, it seemed worth the ride halfway across the country. I thought to myself that this was especially true this year. This land had allowed for some deep personal healing. With all the shake-ups in the early summer, the harrowing plane ride, and Steven's accident, these last few weeks in the peace of the Northwoods brought relief and even some serenity.

Somehow we ended up talking about the history of Hazelhurst, how it had once been completely barren after a logging company had bought up the land. We both expressed our amazement about how resilient nature seemed to be, restoring it to what it is today. At one point I asked him about Szantay's Point. "Listen, Szantay's Point, that seems to be one of the most peaceful spots on the lake, and yet so sad. It looks like there are some ruins over there or something. Do you know anything about it? How come no one's built on it in all these years?"

"Well," the old man said, "no one's built on it because it was donated to the University of Wisconsin. I suppose that's why it's been preserved all these years."

"Did the university begin to build something and then give it up?"

"No. It is a sad story." He stroked his chin with his fingers as he continued, "Actually, a house was never built there, just started. The couple that bought the point years ago sunk all their money into the land, and started to build a mighty fine house right on the top of the hill there, overlooking the water on both sides. It was their dream house for their new life together. You can see a few beautiful stairways heading down to the lake, though they're almost completely covered over by growth now. And that dock, it's where they planned to put their boat in the water. Some people still launch their boats over there today. But the house was never finished because just after they got started, tragedy struck."

"What? Did they lose all their money or something?"

"No. They were both killed," he replied. "Having no children, the property returned to their next of kin, who didn't have the heart to do much of anything with it, being the couple's dream home and all. They ended up donating the land to the university. They thought that would be the best thing."

"How did they die? In a car accident?"

"No. They were both killed in a plane crash."

PART 5

HOME!

21

STILL REACHING

We took our time returning home, spending an evening with friends in Chicago, and also another semi-
restful night in a roadside motel in eastern Ohio.
This gave me some time to mentally and emotionally
absorb all that had happened leading up to Bruce's
appearance.

I felt I had been gently led to a point where I
was able to accept Bruce as a reality in my life, and
also as my big brother rather than the baby he had
been when he passed. I now understood that when
in a state of hypnosis on Dottie's table, when I had
the strange sense that someone wanted to meet me,
that person was not really Lachy, but Bruce. I also
realized that I was led to meet up with an older man
like Lachy so that I could gain a new connection to
Bruce. After all, in my mind Bruce went from being
a helpless child to being a fully grown older brother.
If he had just shown up like that without preparation, I wouldn't have recognized him. He would
have scared me to death! But through this gentle

leading, through contact with Lachy, and mainly through my own struggles to understand the darkness and fear in my own life, I had been prepared to recognize him for who he really was. Because of this knowledge, I was now beginning to understand the fear and the void growing up, now beginning to see past the darkness. I was healing. The real sense of Bruce's presence brought me peace and assurance in the afterlife and the knowledge that loved ones who pass on do not really leave us. We are all connected, bound together by love, fate, and so much more—forever!

It also occurred to me that Bruce's making himself known to me so dramatically in my time of emotional crisis was the equivalent of Lachy's description of the "biggest hand" he'd ever seen pulling him to safety. I liked the idea that Bruce had performed a brilliant rescue mission to save me, offering a hand to lift me out of the firefight over my soul. My personal demons—fear, doubt, grief, loneliness—were in full attack. They had penetrated the perimeter, and I was in trouble. To use Kosan's terminology, it felt as if the lions were closing in for the kill. Bruce swooped down just in time to lift me out of that plight and set me on higher, safer ground. Reflecting on this scenario made me laugh, realizing that on yet another level, he had likely done the exact same thing for Steven! He had caught him up in his arms in the nick of time and gently set him down on safer ground. So many events in the past weeks were taking on much greater meaning, and now seemed beyond coincidence. As in South Africa, I felt as if I was living in some sort of movie. Life had a scripted, surreal quality to it.

I still wondered why everything had happened in the way it did. I realized how much I had benefited from this revelation about Bruce, and I did believe that he needed me to know that he had grown up, and that he was very much a part of my life. That is why he sighed with relief and exclaimed, "Finally you have let me grow up!" But was that it? Was that all he wanted? Perhaps it was. But as I reflected upon these things, I realized that there was obviously more to be accomplished—maybe more for me, but mostly more for him and for our family. I thought of my parents. How much would they benefit from knowing of Bruce's appearance to me? Certainly the impact of Bruce's death on my parents, especially my mother, far outweighed and overshadowed any residual impact it had on me. However, I wasn't about to walk into my mother's home and announce that I just had a visit from her departed son. It could kill her. I also recognized that there was a possibility that maybe this was all in my head, that I had simply just cracked. It didn't feel that way. I actually felt better than I had in years. But these dreams and visions and seeing meaning in random events certainly could be interpreted as delusional. If there was any chance that this wasn't real, I wasn't about to hurt my mother with it. She was hurt enough.

As we returned to our home, to all the familiar sights and sounds, to the un-mowed lawn and the thick, humid air of summer in eastern Pennsylvania, I believed that the recent adventure with all its revelations was over. Whatever the reason for all these remarkable events in the last few weeks, this chapter in my life was coming to a close. I had experienced so much and learned what I needed to learn. Now things would calm down and I could get back to my normal routine, incorporating these new realizations about myself, my brother, my family, and about life in general.

This is what I thought would happen. Someone else had a different idea. What happened next made it clear to me that the story was far from over.

We arrived home at around three in the afternoon, and no sooner did we unpack the car than the boys shot off in different directions to visit their friends. Opening the windows to air out the house, sorting and opening mail, and generally nestling into our home again, I was at peace. Cathy and I both sat at the kitchen table and talked and passed mail back and forth as we unwound. Later that afternoon I mowed the lawn while Cathy did some gardening, and that night we had supper with Steven and Owen. Ronnie and Jason were both still out playing with the friends they hadn't seen in three weeks.

It was around seven o'clock that the phone rang and I answered it. It was a friend of my mother's, Debb Ashton. We talked pleasantries for a minute and I told her that we had just gotten back from a three-week trip and were settling in. She caught me up on all the happenings in town while we were away, and we talked a little bit about our families.

"So, what can I do for you, Debb?" I asked.

"Well, actually, I have something for you. I was going through some of our old files here at home, family pictures and such, and I came across a beautiful picture of your mother and Bruce. It was taken by the hospital when Bruce was born as part of a promotional piece. It's a lovely photo. That's why I saved it. She was and is such a beautiful woman. I don't know if she still has the picture, but I thought I'd pass it along to you."

"A picture of Mom and Bruce together! No, I've never seen it. I'd be delighted to have it. Do you want me to come over and get it?" I was touched by her thinking of me when she found it. It fit so well with all that had happened. Perhaps this photo was another gift from the heavens.

"No, no. I'll swing by tonight or tomorrow morning and drop it off," she replied.

At the time I really didn't think that much more about it, although I did wonder why I had never seen that photo. Was it too much for Mom? Had she put it away forever because it was too painful to keep? Was it hidden away somewhere? How terrible it must have been for her.

That night there were warnings on the television about a strong storm coming in. The wind picked up around ten o'clock, just after the older boys returned home. They wanted to have some of their friends stay overnight, but we turned them down, saying that this being our first night home we needed a little rest. They put up an unusually strong fight, but finally gave in and settled down in the living room to listen to some music and talk.

I felt like releasing some energy, so I went down to our basement to play the drums. We had an old drum set down there, and I wanted to make sure it wasn't sitting in the part of the basement that often flooded during a good rain—the type they were predicting that night. I figured I might as well bang on the drums for a while before I moved them.

After playing the drums for about ten minutes, I moved to a couch that sat directly in front of a second-hand television we'd picked up at a garage sale recently. I was just sitting there with nothing particular on my mind when Steven came bouncing down the stairs and asked if he could play the drums while I sat there. I said that would be fine and he began to bang away. After about five minutes we began to talk. He spoke about his accident and asked if he would ever remember what had happened, because most of it was a blank to him. I told him that he might, but that he shouldn't worry about it.

"Sometimes we forget things so they won't hurt us," I told him. "You'll remember if there is some reason to remember." He seemed satisfied with that answer.

As we sat in silence, I glanced over to the television set and asked Steven, "Should I turn on the television?" Before he could answer me, blip! The television turned on all by itself, right on cue. We both looked at each other in amazement.

"What was that? How did that happen?" Steven asked with his eyes wide open.

I sat up, looking for the remote control that I assumed I would find lying under me, but it wasn't there. I spotted it lying on the floor ten feet away. I didn't have a clue how the television turned itself on. Like a good dad, I wanted to alleviate Steven's concern, so I made up the most logical explanation I could think of. "You know how garage door openers can be on the same frequency? Well, probably it's the same with TVs. Somebody somewhere just turned on their television and it caused ours to go on." In actuality I had never heard of that happening before, and this television was ten feet underground in a basement. But Steven bought the explanation. Why wouldn't he?

I turned the television off and headed upstairs with Steven. I had a funny feeling about this. Not only was it very strange, but it reminded me of something. I couldn't remember what it was, but the scenario seemed familiar: I wanted something to happen and it just happened without me actually physically doing it. When had that happened before? I chalked it up as being some sort of technological freak occurrence.

Cathy was reading on the bed, getting ready to go to sleep for the night. I told her, "Now Cathy, I don't want to say anything about what just happened except to note it, because it was sort of creepy. The television just turned itself on right when I asked Steven if he wanted to watch television." I said no more, and Cathy acted relieved that I wasn't going to say anything else. We both wanted a break from all the strangeness. Still, it happened, and I at least needed to tell her.

That night I went to bed early. The boys were still up watching television, and I didn't bother locking the house, which was out of character for me. In this case, I was just too tired. I fell asleep thinking about the television and wondering what memory it had triggered, nagging me just outside my conscious mind.

At about six o'clock in the morning I awoke to the sound of

the sump pump running in the basement. Apparently we had slept through the storm, but enough rain had gotten into the basement to get that pump running. As I opened my eyes wide and prepared myself to get out of bed and go view the damage, I suddenly had the strangest sense that someone was watching me. I glanced over at the bedroom door, which was partially open, and there I saw what appeared to be a young man staring in the doorway at us. I jumped when I saw him, and he turned and walked quickly down the hall toward the kitchen.

As I scrambled out of bed in my underwear, I thought to myself, *Do I run after him and catch him, or do I put on my pants first?* I knew if I stopped to get dressed he might get away, so I leapt toward the door half naked in hot pursuit. My first thought was that the boys had snuck someone in overnight, and I just wanted to catch him and see who he was. As I followed the boy, he turned the corner into the kitchen. Less than a second later, I turned the same corner. He was gone. There was our dog, who gently lifted his head to greet me and began wagging his tail. The kitchen door that led outside was locked. No one could have gotten out of the kitchen before I came in, and there was no one there.

What had happened? I walked back into the hall and checked both of the boys' rooms. There they were, all bunched up, snoring away. They hadn't snuck anyone in overnight. This was something else.

I thought about it, remembering what had happened the night before. Again, something felt so familiar. It was almost as if these two events were supposed to convey a message. Why a boy in the hall? He had been wearing a red shirt—why did that seem so familiar? How had he disappeared after going into the kitchen? And then there was the television incident. Was someone communicating something?

Having no answers, I went to the basement to check the

flood damage. Turning on the light and heading down into that damp place where the television had popped on the night before brought me a little sense of anxiety. I gently crept halfway down the steps, hoping that the television wouldn't pop on again while I was standing there. I surveyed the room and saw that the water had pretty well kept to the area near the pump and could be cleaned up later. I ran back up the stairs into the bedroom, closed and locked the bedroom door, and got back into bed.

I couldn't sleep. I was scared. I asked God to stop the paranormal incidents. They were too much to handle. Just in case it was Bruce, I asked him too. "Bruce, that's it, man. I can't take anymore. You're scaring me. I don't know what you want me to know or to see, or what you are trying to tell me, but you have to stop."

Suddenly it dawned on me. I realized what seemed so familiar. This was reminding me of the ghost in the New Room!

"The ghost! Of course!" I said to myself, almost breathless at the realization. The television popping on like that, it reminded me of the stereo in the New Room, and how the old ghost used to communicate through it. It was also very similar to the time in Chicago that Cathy had reminded me of after our emergency landing, when I put a CD in the player and asked for number five, and the player accommodated me. What about the CD player going on the fritz while I was with Dottie? And the boy—that also reminded me of a few things. Why was he at the doorway? So many times the ghost in the New Room was seen or was associated with a doorway. The boy was wearing a red shirt, just like the ghost. He didn't look like the man without the face I had seen as a teenager. The boy I'd seen this morning was younger, but he did look like a relative. He had sandy blonde hair and a similar build to my boys. But what could that mean? And the boy running into the kitchen and disappearing—that was similar in ways to the aberration

I saw disappear through the crack in the doorway as my girl-friend and I watched television that night so long ago in my teen years. No, it was not exactly the same, but it was so similar that it made me think. It was almost as if someone wanted me to think about the ghost in the New Room. But why?

I got dressed and walked into the kitchen to make some coffee and think things over. I filled the kettle and put it on the burner and sat down at the table. I wondered again, why would I be pointed back to the ghost in the New Room? If it was Bruce who was behind this paranormal activity—and who else could or would it be—why the ghost in the New Room? I never thought or believed the ghost was associated with him. Bruce was a baby. The ghost was, if you could put an age to him, some-where in his twenties when I was growing up there. That didn't seem right, and what would be the purpose anyway? Why did I need to be nudged and jolted like this? Was there something left to understand? Was there something more for me to do?

I walked over to the stove, poured the hot water into my cup of instant coffee, added sugar and milk, and sat back down at the kitchen table. I took a long sip, reflected once again on these questions, and then set the coffee cup on the table. As I set the cup down I noticed an envelope in front of me. The envelope had a note pasted on it. "For Grant: Here it is." It was the photo of Mom and Bruce! Debb Ashton must have dropped it off the night before. I opened the envelope and pulled out an old eight by ten glossy. There, in the photo, sitting up in bed, was one most beautiful mothers I had ever seen, smiling brightly and proudly, and in her arms rested her baby boy. I was overcome with the sadness and the beauty, the joy that would someday turn to grief.

"Here it is," I repeated to myself. "Here it is." Somehow I knew that I had just received the answer to my question. I was beginning to understand what needed to happen.

22

CONNECTING THE
PIECES

At about nine o'clock that morning I was still thinking about the ghost in the New Room, about my mother, and about all of the strange experiences that had happened. I began to sense that I wanted to talk about this with someone. Just about the time I figured I might give Lachy a call, now that I was back in town, the phone rang. It was Stan Morey, one of my good friends and a member of my men's support group, who had picked me up at the airport a few weeks earlier.

"Grant, welcome back! Listen, I've been talking to Lachy. He's filled me in on your story. Sounds like you've been through a lot lately. I'm going out to breakfast with Lachy in about an hour. We want to know if you want to join us. Any chance?"

"Stan, I was just thinking about calling Lachy. I'd love to get together with you guys. Something's been going on that I need to talk about. How about meeting me over at my office in an hour? I'd like to check in before heading off to breakfast."

"Sure. See ya then."

As I headed over to my office I was excited about having an opportunity to see Lachy again, and also Stan. I trusted these two men completely, and I was eager to share with them what had happened to me the night before and how it fit with everything else that had been happening. I hoped they could help me piece things together. These paranormal happenings were seriously scary. Someone was trying to get my attention. I had the real sense that it was Bruce, or about Bruce, and that perhaps this ghost that had haunted our house was either him or related to him. But this seemed pretty far out. And what did Bruce want me to do with this knowledge anyway?

When I walked into my office and sat down at my desk, I saw the pile of mail my secretary had neatly placed on the corner of the desk. Beside it was a pile of notes with messages about who had called while I was gone. The very top message was written on a full sheet of paper in large print. It simply said, "BRUCE CALLED." I literally flinched when I read it, and for a brief moment wondered whether I was dreaming. Or had my brother now mastered using the phone and was contacting me via the long-distance company's "Friends and Family Plan"?

"What on earth is this?" I exclaimed out loud. Obviously it wasn't my brother, but what did it mean? It seemed like someone was playing a trick on me. It wasn't until the next morning that I found out from my secretary that an old friend named Bruce, someone I hadn't seen in ten years, had called to ask me if I'd marry him and his fiancée. He had told her to simply leave the message that Bruce called, and that he would call back.

Lachy and Stan banged on my door soon after this little coincidence, or rather, cosmic practical joke. We greeted each other with bear hugs. It was good see Lachy again, and his strong and hardy embrace brought me a deep sense of inner comfort. There was that deep connection again! He was the closest thing I had to an older brother in this world, and it felt wonderful. I was happy to see both of them. We chatted for a while and then hopped into Lachy's car and headed off to a local diner for breakfast. In the diner we sat down and talked for close to two hours.

I had a lot to share. I filled them in on the experiences in the Northwoods, and then launched into the topic of my recent encounters with the paranormal, the ghost in the New Room, and how it seemed he was trying to tell me something. Lachy and Stan were fascinated, and immediately began trying to help me solve the mystery.

"Maybe this is part of this sense of urgency you felt when under hypnosis," Stan suggested. "Do you think that was Bruce?"

"I do, but I'm not sure what he is trying to tell me now. The television turning off and on was certainly related to the stereo in the New Room and to the CD player putting on song number five for me. And the boy running down the hall and into the kitchen, that seems related to the New Room too. But why a boy? Why point me there?" I wondered.

"Grant, you talked about needing some support when you put that CD in the machine and wanted to hear number five. Maybe Bruce was the one who put that song on for you. You said that you were lonely and needed help. Why not Bruce?" Lachy asked.

"What CD was it? Did you say it was the soundtrack from the movie *The Mission*? Wooooh. There's a connection. *The Mission!*" Stan added with feigned awe. We laughed. "I've got that CD," he recalled. "It's beautiful, especially 'Gabriel's Oboe.' What's number five called? I don't recall."

"I don't know. I never look at the names of the songs. I just put the CD on and when I like a song I see what number is playing on the machine. Is it possible all these paranormal experiences were Bruce? I just don't know!"

I paused in deep reflection, and Lachy and Stan gave me that space as we sat in silence. Looking deep within, I thought to myself, *Maybe it really was Bruce. I don't know. It does make sense. The main characteristic of this ghost in the New Room was that it was sad, really sad, and it wanted to manifest. The presence would become so strong that I would have to leave the room for fear it was going to appear. Man, to think it was Bruce who wanted to come to me! My brother that close to me for so long, or at least some part of him, hanging on to reach out to me?* The thought was overwhelming, and I held back tears. No wonder this sad presence was the strongest around Christmastime. Here we had everyone's stockings hung up except Bruce's, all the gifts and everything, and not a mention of him. Maybe Bruce was crying out, "Don't forget about me. Remember me!" It now made sense that my parents sat there silent on Christmas morning with painted smiles while we opened our gifts. Bruce was in their minds and hearts. My mother hid the awful grief at that time, but the grief was so huge that it personified!

Lachy's voice broke the silence. "I don't know." He paused for a moment of reflection. "You said you saw someone in the doorway—a man with a red shirt and no face. How does that fit in?"

"That doesn't seem to make sense. Why was it a man? Bruce was a kid!" I responded.

Lachy interrupted. "No. You just got finished saying that you've discovered that Bruce is grown up. How old was the man in the doorway? In his twenties." We stopped speaking as Lachy and I both looked at each other and started counting on our fingers at the same time. If Bruce had lived, he would have been in his twenties during my adolescent years.

"He would have been twenty. Bingo!" Lachy announced.

"Yes, you know, it all fits. But why didn't he have a face?

That doesn't make much sense." I was still having a hard time relating this specter to Bruce, having never considered the possibility in all of my years.

"Of course he didn't have a face. You didn't know him. Whether he was a real ghost or just some sort of representation of Bruce, he was faceless because he was ignored, or maybe even erased from your family's consciousness. At least, that sounds like what you're saying," Stan apologetically hypothesized.

"Whoa! That's crazy, but may just be true. He didn't have a face because we didn't recognize him." I reflected on the fact that I had also dreamed about this man on the airplane back from South Africa. My first impression had been that he was a monstrous ghoul haunting my nightmare that terrible night. But no. He had offered support in that dream. In fact, he had offered his arm to me, to give me comfort, to lift me out of my fear. He reminded me so much of my father, or, come to think of it, just an older relative, like a brother. Stirring from these thoughts, I shook my head and reminded myself that it was just a dream that night. But dreams have meaning. Even if this faceless man was only a projection of my own unconscious, of the reality of someone I could sense but could not see, this was a profound discovery for my personal growth.

There were so many theories about what this ghost could have been. Perhaps all of them were true. The ghost was the unspoken grief, the ghost was a projection of my longing to understand the missing person in the family, the ghost was, indeed, Bruce. Or, at the very least, I had an intriguing story to tell—a story with so much adventure, so much mystery, so many challenges, so many discoveries and opportunities for healing, that it had to be told to others. It was too incredible to keep to myself. But I still wondered why I needed to know these things. "Why do you think Bruce wants me to link him with the ghost in the New Room?" I asked them.

"Grant, maybe you were led to us to help you out, because sometimes I think you're pretty stupid." Lachy said the words with a smile, patting me on the back. "When the boy ran into the kitchen he was leading you somewhere. What did you find in there? You found a picture of your mother holding Bruce. The freaking envelope even said, 'Here it is.' What more do you want?" Lachy asked in a sort of sarcastic, big-brother tone.

"You mean he wants me to know that this is about my mother?" I asked, still perplexed.

"Maybe he wants you to talk to her. Maybe it's over for you, but it isn't over for her," he responded.

I knew that he was right. I had sensed this ever since Bruce appeared to me in the cabin in the Northwoods, but I was afraid. I knew I had to talk to her when I saw that picture of her and her baby boy. I realized that I should probably talk to the whole family, or at least Beth Ann, who remembered Bruce.

"You're right, Lachy! I knew that was the answer. It's just that it terrifies me to think that I have to open up old wounds in the family. Whatever I say is going to kill my mom."

"I don't know. It's going to hurt, but it could be the beginning of some needed healing."

"And don't forget," Stan added, "Bruce is going to heal too. Maybe that's the most important thing of all, because it seems like he's gone to a lot of trouble to get this message through to you. He needs it too."

"Yeah, but how? How do I introduce this subject? I don't want to just walk in on Mom and drop this on her. Maybe I could send a letter..."

"Get serious, Grant. You can't send a letter," Lachy responded.

"Yeah, of course I can't. But maybe I can read something to her. I took some notes about my dream of Bruce. Maybe I could write a little poem. I think she'd listen to a poem about him. Writing it would also be therapeutic for me. What do you think?" I asked.

"It might work. But you definitely need to warn her it's coming. She needs to be ready to hear it," Stan added.

We finished up our conversation and Lachy offered to pay the bill. They dropped me off at my office and we agreed that we would get together again and talk about this later.

That afternoon I wrote a few pages about my encounter with Bruce in the Northwoods and what it meant to me to know that I had an older brother. What I wrote was somewhere between poetry and prose. The artistic side of me wasn't very pleased with it, but the emotional side loved it. I wrote about being a boy and feeling all alone, and how beautiful it was to discover my brother. I wanted so much to share it with the family, especially with my mother. But I thought I'd first try it out on Beth Ann. Something was left undone in our last conversation together, and I could sense her deep pain. She would benefit from talking about Bruce.

Later that afternoon, I paid Beth Ann a visit.

"I think I know why you are here." She seemed much calmer than the last time I saw her. She had a sense of peace about her, and openness. "You want to talk about Bruce."

"How did you know?" I asked.

"Well, I know that you have been thinking about him lately. I think we all have."

"You're right, Beth Ann. I've been thinking about him a lot." It didn't take long for me to open up to Beth Ann and tell her about what had happened in the past few weeks. She listened intently and with care. I read her the sketchy poem I had written, and she shed a few tears. Then she opened up.

"I knew something was happening because I had a dream about him too, just about the same time you did. It might have even been on the same day. Sometimes I really do feel him, and

I think he's with me. It certainly seems real and comforting, but I don't like to make too much of it. I haven't told anyone about this.... You know, when he died he just disappeared..." She started to cry. "No one told me what happened. He just went away and never came back. I kept waiting for him to come back, but he never did. I knew people were sad, but I didn't know why." She paused and wiped her eyes.

"That's terrible, Beth Ann. You were only four years old. You must have felt so frightened and alone, powerless! You've been holding on to a lot, haven't you?"

She frowned like a little girl. "Yes. I've been holding on ever since it happened—maybe to the hope that someday he would come back. I don't know. I think something deep inside me has been waiting for some resolution to this all my life." The frown passed and she managed a modest smile. "I wondered why Bruce has seemed so much closer to me in the past few weeks. He's been wanting to be recognized, to gain his rightful place in the family—at least in our memory." She paused in deep thought and then continued. "Maybe this is the beginning. Maybe we can finally let him be a real part of the family. Maybe we can finally let him come home!" We held each other and cried.

"I am going to go home and call Mom. I'm going to ask her if I can come over and read her the poem," I calmly announced to Beth Ann. Inside I shuddered at the thought, but I knew I had to do it.

"She's going to be upset," Beth Ann replied. "I'm not making you do this. You're doing this of your own free will!" she half joked.

"Yes, I am afraid to do this. I don't want to hurt her. But I think Bruce needs this, and I think it will help her too, and all of us." I imagined facing my mother with this painful subject, and I whispered to myself, "Hoka hey!" I knew that this would be running into the roar and facing my fears. But the more I thought about it, I realized I didn't need to do this for me. I needed to do this for Mom and for Bruce.

Beth Ann and I talked a little while longer and then we said goodbye. We knew this wasn't the end but the beginning of a long process of healing. Both of us commented that we could feel a weight lifting from us. A cloud that surrounded us for so long was quickly dissipating. As I hurried home to call my mother, I hoped this healing would come to her as well.

As I walked into the house Cathy greeted me with wide eyes and a big smile. I wondered at this. She seemed so light and happy, like a little girl on her birthday. "What is up with you?" I asked.

"Oh, I had a little visit," she coyly replied. "You know, you're not the only one who has paranormal experiences. I just had a doozy this morning, and I'm just going to enjoy it. I don't have to analyze it and all that, like some people I know," she chided me with a look.

"What? Come on! What happened?" I asked, really curious by this time.

"I now believe something is happening, Grant. I'm not sure what, but I cannot doubt that somehow the spiritual world is moving closer to us. I heard his voice clear as day, and I have no doubt it was him," she said with girlish pride.

"Who?" I asked. "Your father?"

"Yes, Daddy," she declared with a smile. "I was working in the garden and I was thinking about all these paranormal events, and about your brother and family. Then I started reflecting on my family and how much Mom must miss Daddy. Then, I guess because of everything we've been talking about, I wondered whether Daddy missed her too, seeing that he's in heaven and all that. Then, with that thought, out of the blue and clear as day, I heard his voice. He asked, 'What does she smell like?' Can you believe that?"

"'What does she smell like?' What does that mean?" I wondered.

"It was sort of in a reminiscent way, sort of like he was reflecting about her and remembering her touch and her smell when he lived here with her. I suppose he missed that smell." Tears formed in Cathy's eyes.

"I suppose he does miss that." I put my arms around her and held her. "Did you answer him?" I asked.

"What? No," she replied. "It was a rhetorical question."

As we stood in the living room and held each other, we both thought of how a few weeks ago we stood on the other side of the world in each other's arms, frightened and feeling so vulnerable and alone. So much had happened since then. It was so good to be home and be together again, and have a lifetime to figure it all out. All these things that were happening, these revelations, these gentle whispers from above, the angelic touch of love, we knew it wouldn't last forever. This window to the other world would soon close. And we were glad. We didn't have the stamina to take much more of it. We both sensed that we had received what we needed for healing. It truly was a new beginning.

Not five minutes after our conversation about Cathy's beautiful experience of hearing her father's voice, just as I was about to pick up the phone to call my mother, the phone rang. It was a very excited Stan Morey.

"Grant. Hi. Do you still own the soundtrack of *The Mission?*" he asked breathlessly.

"Yeah, it's probably somewhere. Why?" I asked.

"Well, you might want to look at the names of the songs."

"What do you mean?"

"After our conversation this morning I just had to listen to that CD again. I forgot how good it is. I just finished listening to it. Anyway, what song did you say you liked to listen to?

The one that would bring you comfort? You know, the one your brother put on for you?"

"Number five. Why?"

"Well, Grant, maybe this doesn't mean a thing, but with everything that has happened, it's one more piece of the puzzle for you. Do you know what number five on that CD is called?"

"No. What?"

"'Brothers'!"

23

REUNITED

"Hello?"

"Mom, it's me. How are you?"

"Oh, I am so glad you're back. Are the boys all right? How's Steven?"

"Everybody is fine, Mom. We had a wonderful time. I'd love to tell you all about it. But I'm calling you now because something remarkable happened, and I need to talk to you about it." I could feel my stomach begin to tense up with these words. There was no turning back now. I had committed to face the potential roar of the lions.

"What about? This isn't anything about what had happened, is it? I don't think I can take any more. I can only hold on so long. It's not about the accident, is it?" She didn't speak from anger, it seemed, but rather from fear. I sensed a slight quiver in her voice. This gave me pause. I didn't want to go on with this. I didn't want to hurt her or bring her any pain. But then I realized I had to. I had to for me, for Bruce, but maybe most of all for her.

"No, Mom. It's about Bruce." Silence. Deafening silence. I sensed the darkness closing in on this conversation. Was she crying? In pain? Was she so angry she couldn't speak? Then I heard her let out a long breath. Her response surprised me, and made me wonder whether she, too, hadn't been in some way prepared for this.

"OK. Do you want to come over and talk to me?" she asked in an acquiescent tone of voice—a tone I had rarely, if ever, heard from her. "What is it about?"

"I had a dream about Bruce, and sort of a vision, and I wrote a poem I want to share with you."

Again, silence on the other end, and a sigh. Then, in a gentle, little girl's voice, she asked, "Is it going to make me cry?"

"Yes. It is going to make us both cry."

Silence. The little girl said, "OK. Come on over."

I ran out the door just as soon as I hung up the phone. My mother lived not more than three minutes away on foot, and I wanted to get over there as quickly as humanly possible. I felt that the less time I gave her or myself, the less chance there was that one of us would change our minds. Catching my breath on her porch, I knocked on the door, entered, and found her sitting at the table in the kitchen. I hugged and kissed her, and sat down opposite her.

"Mom, I had a dream that Bruce came to me."

She looked at me sternly. "Oh, stop it, Grant!"

"No. He did. In my dream he was older than me. He was my big brother."

She turned away. "Why are you doing this to me? I have had to carry this for so long and have been so alone. I've done a good job. I don't need this."

"Maybe you don't need this, but maybe I do, and maybe Bruce does."

Turning to face me, she calmed down a little, but her voice

was still pained. "What's the purpose in bringing up this pain? We can't bring him back."

"No, but maybe we can let him go. Maybe if we let go of the old pain, he can be with us in a new way. I saw him, Mom. I swear it was real. I didn't ask for him to come to me. He came on his own. He needed me to know that he was my big brother, and that a day hasn't gone by that he hasn't been with me. I'm sure it's the same with you, even more so. Maybe that's what he wants you to know. I don't know. I just want to read you this poem. That's all."

"How can you believe? How can you have such faith?" She paused, processing what I had said. "You said he was older? Is this in your dream?"

"I think the poem will explain, Mom. At least it will explain what I've been going through, and what healing I've received. You know I've needed it so badly after Steven's accident and the emergency landing. I think reading this to you will help me at the very least, and maybe it will do some good for you too. I don't know." I began to wonder whether I had made a mistake in coming. Why did I need to do this? Why was I putting her through so much pain? What good could possibly come of it?

"All right. I'd like to hear your poem. I want to hear it.... Wait." She settled herself into the seat and gave a very light shake of her head as if to clear it. Then she fixed her gaze on the window across from us and waited for me to begin.

"It's a long poem. It's not very good. It's sort of a story and..."

"I'm sure it's fine. Go ahead." Like I was her little boy back in elementary school again, she encouraged me to stop putting myself down and to share what I had created.

"OK. It's titled 'For Bruce.'" I gathered my senses and began to read.

When I was a young man
I walked alone in deep forests
Where the wind tickled the trees,
And the sunlight danced on mossy ground.
Drinking silent stillness of flowing brooks,
Rolling in the warm grass to the bottom of the hill,
Stopping, face down, to breathe in the scent of the earth's rich soil.
My thoughts were my only companion,
And hopes of meadows and gentle turns in the stream.
Yet fears of footsteps often pushed me on.

Sometimes in my seclusion,
I would stumble upon a vision,
And in my imagining mind,
The path would find a clearing and a boy so young.
I saw him on the quiet path,
Squatting upright beside the waters,
Bare arms and chest, his little body bent over the edge,
Gazing down, outward, and beyond.
Though he did not see me,
Because our worlds could never touch,
Barred by the lines of earthly days,
Separated at that point where life and death meet,
I could imagine him there, and behold his face and eyes,
Which so quietly stared off into distant horizons.

"Mom, I was thinking about that picture you showed me of him in the baby pool. You know the one. He had that faraway look in his eyes. That's where I got that image."

"Yes, I see. It's a beautiful poem."

"Thank you. I'll go on." I returned to the poem where I had left off.

As I reached for him
He turned and walked away,
Leaving behind not the slightest footprint,
The little boy disappeared into the darkness.
And I heard my father's tears falling,
As he tried not to openly cry.
My mother's sorrowful groan echoed in the valleys.
Like distant thunder it faded into the silence.
They buried him in his little cowboy boots and his best suit.

With those words we both sobbed. My mother got up, hurried over to the counter to retrieve a box of tissues, and returned to hand me one. I read on with my nose half clogged and tears streaming down my eyes.

I hacked my way through the thick vines
Of entangled thoughts and fears,
I hid beneath the fallen trees at night,
While monsters roamed the shadow world
In search of my soul.
My belief in God gave me no relief.
Though I saw him as my friend,
At night he seemed so far away,
As far away as my brother:
Too high in the heavens to see me,
Too young and fragile to care,
Too far away to be more than an old photograph
In my mother's dresser drawer,
And so few words.

I paused for a moment. "I'm sorry, Mom. It's just that I didn't know much about him."

"It's all right. We didn't have many pictures. I wish we had more.... There are so many things I wish I did when I look back. But it's too late now.... Go on. Read the poem."

"OK." The poem went on to explain that years went by, and I grew to an adult, having my own children. I spoke about how much I longed for their brotherhood, and spoke of the special sweat lodge with them down by the lake when they prayed with such innocence and trust in God.

Emerging from our mother's womb,
Hot steam escaping as they crawled out under the stars,
They walked into the still lake and up to their heads.
They swam in the silence of the night.
Though they called to me
I waited on the shoreline,
The brave warrior who so deeply shivered inside
Under the fallen trees, a boy still.

As I stood knee-deep on the edge of their dreams,
I saw my life as too many days of solitude,
Too many times I stopped short on the shoreline,
Too many times I halted my path along the way,
Afraid to turn the bend and see his little face of concern gazing at me,
That potential specter just ahead caused me too much terror,
Like the monsters' search for my soul.
In fear I ran from his face,
The face of my brother,
Who left me before I was born.

A day passed, or two, from this gathering,
And in the quiet of the lonely night:
Dreams....
As a very little boy I stood by the brook I had seen so long ago.
I heard the strong voice behind me,
Of a man who walked my trodden path.
He called to me, "Little brother!"
As I turned and looked up at this man,
He smiled with a love and warmth so deep,

The kindness in his way
Confirmed to me that he was my brother.
Bone of my bone, flesh of my flesh—brother.

"Now the next part, Mom, really happened. OK? I mean I wasn't dreaming, and the more I've reflected on it the more I realize how miraculous it was. I'll continue."

I awoke, realizing I was not alone,
I cried before the bathroom mirror.
I saw my twisted, red-faced little boy's eyes
Stream with tears.
I shared with that boy the good and surprising news,
"I HAVE a brother!"
"I have a BIG brother!"
As I wiped the last tears from my cheeks,
As plain as day, and as awake as I could be,
The darkness I feared so much gently entered that room,
Becoming a human being, he sat beside me.
"Finally you have let me grow up!
"I have always been your big brother.
"I have always been with you.
"And I always will be."

Another night passed,
The hissing rocks burned hot in my lodge,
And the spitting water spoke
Of new courage and dreams.
Springing from the lodge to the dark waters before me,
I swam over my head:
Baptized with new courage and resolve,
Floating back to the shore I stood and gazed upward.
An eagle cried on a distant shore.
Two brothers stood side by side on that beach,
And stared into the stars.

The poem was over. By this time, my mother and I were both sobbing and passing the box of tissues between us. We cried in silence, without a word, for several minutes. I can only describe it as a very deep and sweet moment of release.

"Do you think he really came to you?" she asked, wiping her nose one more time.

"I don't know. How could I doubt? So many things have been happening. So many strange coincidences and other things. I think he needed me to tell you. He wanted me to tell you. And I would never have dared talk about this if it wasn't for him. Yes. I do believe."

My mother broke into tears again, and then cried openly. This was something I had never heard or seen before. "I am so sorry. I wanted to talk about it. I didn't mean to leave all of you in the dark. The pain I carried! The pain!" I could hear years of grief pouring out of her voice.

"It's OK, Mom, you did the best you could."

"You know, I used to be a happy person, but that all changed when Bruce died. It changed my life forever. I was shocked. I was crushed.... You don't get over the death of a child. I wanted so much to talk about it, but I couldn't. Your father's such a strong man, but he's not very talkative. You know he wasn't raised with a lot of compassion, so he didn't always show so much of it. We did talk some. But it was awful. I was so young. And when Bruce died I went to my father for help." She paused and shivered with those words like a little girl left out in the cold. As she tried to speak she choked on her tears. She cried for a few minutes and then, composing herself until she only had occasional sobs, she continued.

"There was something wrong with the autopsy report. I don't know what it was. But I went to my father and I asked him if he could help me and take a look at it. I held out the paper.... I just wanted some help from my father...." Her small voice trembled. "He pushed it away and told me, 'I don't want to talk about it!' He walked away from me. I almost died.... My own father!" She cried again.

"Did he ever talk to you about Bruce?"

"Never. It wasn't his way. That's how a lot of people did things back then. They just sucked it up and held it in. That's eventually what I ended up doing. I figured that was the only way. No one knew any differently at that time."

"Oh, Mom. I had no idea." I tried to think of words to console her.

She continued, "I often wondered why my father wouldn't talk about it, and I learned from my mother that my father had a brother who died when he was three years old. Perhaps it brought back too much pain for him."

"Did you talk to anyone? There were no support groups back then, were there? How about your friends? Someone? I suppose it was a different time."

"Well, some of my friends lost children too. I suppose we talked a little, but I didn't want to impose on them. They had their own troubles."

"How about professional help? Did you see anyone?"

"No one. Well, one very young minister came over and he tried, but he just didn't say what I needed to hear at the time. In fact, all I wanted was someone to give me permission to cry, but he didn't do that. He said that I should be happy." She shook with grief as even more tears flooded from her eyes. "He said that Bruce was an angel now and that I should be thrilled, and be proud of him. I just wanted to die. Even if it was true, it wasn't what I needed to hear."

"What minister would do that? Who was it?" I became angry and indignant.

"No." With motherly mercy, Mom refused to tell me who it was. "He really had such an innocent and strong faith in the afterlife. And his faith was tested in a terrible way. You see, he also lost his son. His son was taken from him years later. He was killed in Vietnam. When his son died he managed to hold on to that innocent faith. He told people how proud he was that his son was a hero, and that he knew that his son was in heaven. I don't blame him for anything."

"His son died in Vietnam?"

"Yes. He was a true war hero, and his father was so proud of him. He was killed as he tried to rescue others in his squad. He had saved most of them, but then when he went back to retrieve the last one, he was killed."

"Was his name Rick?" I asked in astonishment.

"Yes. How did you know?"

"I just heard all about him. His brother just shared the whole story. Funny how these things happen."

"Yes. Funny." Mom sat in deep reflection. I thought to myself, *Could this simply be another coincidence? It all seemed to be planned by someone for some incredible reason.*

"I wanted to talk about it, or to do something to help cope," she said in a philosophical tone as her tears were drying. "But I didn't know what to do, so I just put my grief away, out of sight. There wasn't a day that went by that I didn't grieve, but I hid it. And you never recover, you know. It feels like yesterday even now."

"I can imagine."

"Yes. And I thought about what we could do to remember Bruce. I thought that maybe we could set up a place setting for him at the dinner table, something like that to remember him." She glanced up into my eyes for approval. "But that would be too much. Wouldn't that have been too much?"

"Yeah. That would have been too much."

"I thought about maybe putting up a stocking at Christmas or something. At Christmastime it was so bad. I could hardly open the gifts. And those fights we all used to have. It was the tension. The darkness was so great, but I never spoke about it. I kept it in. Like the good little girl my father always insisted I be, I kept it inside, and no one knew." We both broke into tears again, and I put my arm around her. Now I knew why the darkness was so strong at Christmastime. I knew for certain now that the haunting in that house was precipitated by her unspoken grief. Now the grief was releasing, and the ghost, of whatever nature or origin, was being set free.

"Bruce, I am so sorry," she cried. "I love you."

As we both held each other and cried, I sensed that something even more wonderful, even more precious, was happening. I could swear I sensed there was another person with us. I heard another voice crying very gently even as we cried. Was it my imagination? Was it Bruce? I didn't know. But we were not alone in that kitchen. I remembered the time, right after Steven was hit by the bus, when something inside, a little boy inside of me, maybe Bruce trying to grow up, begged me to grieve. "Cry for me," he said. Perhaps he had been begging that from each of us? Was it Bruce who now could cry with us because finally we were able to cry for him? Would he now be recognized in our family, given his place, released to go on his way by my mother's own release of her grief? I immediately knew that it was true. I felt that it was true. And as I strained to hear that third person cry, I thought at first it was the sound of a little boy. As I listened more carefully, I realized it was not a boy who cried, but a man. I knew his tears were no longer tears of grief. They were tears of joy. Very quietly, as our crying diminished and our tears dried, I could hear his voice fade away into the distance and disappear beyond the darkness of that place and into the light beyond.

At that moment I realized the fear that plagued me for so long was gone. I no longer sensed the shadows just beyond my sight. They were no more. That void of knowledge had been filled. The questions were all being answered. Even those questions I couldn't put into words as a child were being answered without words, on some cellular level. Somehow it wasn't just Bruce getting off the hook. I was, too. Being the second son, being even for a moment second in importance to my mother, who now grieved openly for her oldest son, I was free! I wasn't the most important person in the world, the one who had to be cared for and worried about, the one who wasn't allowed to die. What was death, anyway, now that Bruce had become so real, now that he had showed himself to us, not only in dreams and visions, not only in paranormal experiences, but even more so in this incredible series of serendipitous events? I was free. Having faced the lions, I had escaped them. And their roars were nothing but empty threats from the unconscious world of childhood fears now exposed and released.

As my mother and I continued our conversation, I could see her complexion lighten up. There is no such thing as instantaneous salvation in matters such as these. Her healing was far from over, and, like she said, you never get over the death of a child. However, I could see clearly that her healing had truly begun, and it brought me such peace and happiness. Perhaps that's all Bruce ever wanted. Mom, Dad, and Beth Ann all needed to talk and to grieve. The rest of us needed to understand. Now that this had begun, Bruce could truly move on. If angels have wings, he earned them that summer. But I suppose he already had them, carrying his nephew to safety in his flight of forty-eight feet.

My mother wiped her tears. "I haven't cried like that in years. I suppose that's what you were aiming for, huh?"

"No. Not really. I didn't know what I wanted. But I hope this was good for you."

"I suppose so. But the grief in there feels limitless. I suppose you have to start somewhere."

"Yeah."

"I wish we had acknowledged Bruce more in the family. I want you to know, though, that I did think about him every day. And though I never spoke about it, I did watch him grow up."

"What do you mean?"

"I mean, I watched his classmates as they grew. I saw them on their way to school. I watched them in the school plays, the sports programs, as they grew and became adults. I would think about Bruce and how he would be their friend and how they would walk together all those days growing up. I watched him grow through them."

"That sounds like it was a good thing for you. Who was in his class? I mean, who did you watch? Was it anyone I know?" Her answer confirmed to me that everything up to this point had not been a series of coincidences, but rather some incredible spiritual force that guided all our paths into one for some greater purpose.

"You know him," she responded. "Lachy Brown."

ADDENDUM

More than a decade has passed since I originally wrote this story down. In that time, many things have changed. My mother and father have both passed away. Steven is now in his midtwenties and just returned from a year's adventure in Thailand. I quit the job that called for so much flying and have had a series of several pastoral jobs in my hometown church here in Pennsylvania. I can't say I have had any more spiritual experiences with Bruce like I did that strange summer. I don't need to, I suppose. Bruce is as close as my heart. That's what I have learned.

As for Lachy and me, we have become best friends. We formed a loose-knit organization together, with several others, called Spiritual Alliance to help foster people's desire to live with more love and integrity. As part of this effort, we run a program for young and not-so-young men from suburbia to halfway houses in the Philadelphia area called Spiritual Warfare Effectiveness Training, or SWET for short. We help men fight and overcome their addictive natures and learn to be happy and productive citizens of our world.

Several years ago one of the young men who went through our SWET program and become an integral part of it joined the US Army and was killed in action in the Taji province of Iraq. His name was Tristan Smith. He was the son of a childhood friend of mine, and was truly a fifth son to me. I gave Tristan's memorial address to nearly a thousand community members, firefighters, and soldiers at our hometown church here in Pennsylvania. Tristan's commander at Fort Hood heard the address and asked me to come to Texas and address the troops there about Tristan and the other brave soldiers who had fallen with him. I hadn't flown in years, but I had to go. Tristan's father agreed to go too, and I asked Lachy if he would accompany me on the plane. I knew if Tristan had given his life to serve his country, I had to overcome my fear and get on a plane to honor him and to speak to the brave men and women of the 4th Infantry at Fort Hood.

With Tristan's father and Lachy by my side, we flew down, and I addressed the troops in a powerful memorial service for all those who had fallen in Iraq that month. It seemed like a dream to be on a plane with the man I had grown to respect as my big brother, and to be honoring another son of the nation who had fallen. I felt I had faced the lions.

After the talk, we wandered over to the park in the middle of the base to kill some time before going out to dinner and then leaving for home. As the home of the 4th Infantry and the 9th Cavalry, they had several tanks and old choppers on display in the grassy fields there. Lachy wandered over to a Cobra helicopter and asked if I would take his picture next to it. He said this was just like the one he had flown in Vietnam. I took the picture. Lachy said, "This is eerie, but this looks exactly like the chopper I flew in Vietnam. I mean exactly. I'm getting the serial number and I'm going to look this up." We flew home, and Lachy looked it up. You can guess what happened. Yes. That was the chopper he flew in Vietnam.